HARRIS
VERSUS
TRUMP
America's Existential Futures

Other World Scientific Titles by the Authors

America's Future: Biden and the Progressives
ISBN: 978-981-12-5244-0
ISBN: 978-981-12-5334-8 (pbk)

Beleaguered Superpower: Biden's America Adrift
ISBN: 978-981-12-3618-1
ISBN: 978-981-12-3657-0 (pbk)

Populists and Progressives: The New Forces in American Politics
ISBN: 978-981-12-1718-0
ISBN: 978-981-12-1840-8 (pbk)

The Trump Phenomenon and the Future of US Foreign Policy
ISBN: 978-981-320-087-6
ISBN: 978-981-320-099-9 (pbk)

HARRIS VERSUS TRUMP

America's Existential Futures

Steven Rosefielde
University of North Carolina, Chapel Hill, USA

Daniel Quinn Mills
Harvard Business School, USA

NEW JERSEY · LONDON · SINGAPORE · BEIJING · SHANGHAI · HONG KONG · TAIPEI · CHENNAI

Published by

World Scientific Publishing Co. Pte. Ltd.
5 Toh Tuck Link, Singapore 596224
USA office: 27 Warren Street, Suite 401-402, Hackensack, NJ 07601
UK office: 57 Shelton Street, Covent Garden, London WC2H 9HE

British Library Cataloguing-in-Publication Data
A catalogue record for this book is available from the British Library.

HARRIS VERSUS TRUMP
America's Existential Futures

Copyright © 2025 by World Scientific Publishing Co. Pte. Ltd.

All rights reserved. This book, or parts thereof, may not be reproduced in any form or by any means, electronic or mechanical, including photocopying, recording or any information storage and retrieval system now known or to be invented, without written permission from the publisher.

For photocopying of material in this volume, please pay a copying fee through the Copyright Clearance Center, Inc., 222 Rosewood Drive, Danvers, MA 01923, USA. In this case permission to photocopy is not required from the publisher.

ISBN 978-981-98-0564-8 (hardcover)
ISBN 978-981-98-0629-4 (paperback)
ISBN 978-981-98-0565-5 (ebook for institutions)
ISBN 978-981-98-0566-2 (ebook for individuals)

For any available supplementary material, please visit
https://www.worldscientific.com/worldscibooks/10.1142/14110#t=suppl

Desk Editor: Jiang Yulin

Typeset by Stallion Press
Email: enquiries@stallionpress.com

Printed in Singapore

About the Authors

Steven Rosefielde, Professor of Economics, University of North Carolina, Chapel Hill, received his PhD from Harvard University and is a Member of the Russian Academy of Natural Sciences (RAEN). His books include: *Democracy and Its Elected Enemies: The West's Paralysis, Crisis and Decline*, Cambridge University Press, 2013; *Inclusive Economic Theory* (with Ralph W. Pfouts), World Scientific Publishers, 2014; *Global Economic Turmoil and the Public Good* (with Quinn Mills), World Scientific Publishers, 2015; *Transformation and Crisis in Central and Eastern Europe: Challenges and Prospects* (with Bruno Dallago), Routledge, 2016; *Kremlin Strikes Back: Russia and the West after Crimea's Annexation*, Cambridge University Press, 2017; *The Trump Phenomenon and Future of US Foreign Policy* (with Quinn Mills), World Scientific Publishers, 2016; *Trump's Populist America*, World Scientific Publishers, 2017; *China's Market Communism: Challenges, Dilemmas, Solutions* (with Jonathan Leightner), Routledge, 2017; *The Unwinding of the Globalist Dream: EU, Russia, China* (with Masaaki Kuboniwa, Kumiko Haba and Satoshi Mizobata, eds.), World Scientific Publishers, 2017; *Putin's Russia: Economic, Political and Military Foundations*, World Scientific Publishers, 2020; *Socialist Economic Systems: 21st Century Pathways*, Routledge, 2023; *Russo-Ukrainian War: Implications for the Asia Pacific*, World Scientific Publishers, 2023; *Beleaguered Superpower: America Adrift* (with Quinn Mills), World Scientific Publishers, 2022.

Daniel Quinn Mills provides thought leadership in several fields including leadership, strategy, economics and geopolitics. He has been a director of publicly listed firms and is currently a director of several closely held private corporations. He has published books about business activities, the media, American foreign policy, economic policy, and political processes.

During the Viet Nam War, Mills spent several years in Washington, D.C. helping to control inflation. For several years, he was in charge of all wages, prices and profits in the construction industry (then 14% of GDP). Simultaneously, he taught at MIT's Sloan School of Management. Thereafter, he taught at the Harvard Business School. He has done consulting and speaking in the following countries: United States, Canada, the United Kingdom, Indonesia, Ireland, France, the Netherlands, Germany, Switzerland, Italy, Russia, Israel, China, Japan, Malaysia, Brazil, Colombia, Mexico, Singapore, South Africa, Kuwait, the United Arab Emirates, Saudi Arabia, Vietnam and Australia.

Mills earned his MA and PhD from Harvard, both in economics. He received his undergraduate degree from Ohio Wesleyan.

Throughout his career, Mills has been an influential author. His most recent books are *Authoritarians Resurgent: Rethinking Global Security* (with Steven S. Rosefielde) forthcoming; *The Trump Phenomenon and the Future of US Foreign Policy* (with Steven S. Rosefielde), 2016; *Global Economic Turmoil and the Public Good* (with Steven S. Rosefielde), 2015; *Shadows of the Civil War*, 2014; *The Leader's Guide to Past and Future*, 2013; *Democracy and Its Elected Enemies* (with Steven S. Rosefielde), 2013; *The Financial Crisis of 2008–'10*, 2010; and *Rising Nations* (with Steven S. Rosefielde), 2009. Previously he published *Masters of Illusion: Presidential Leadership, Strategic Independence and America's Public Culture* (with Steven S. Rosefielde), 2007.

Preface

American presidential election campaigns are supposed to inform the public about present dangers and opportunities, enabling voters to choose the candidate most likely to defend the quality of national existence.

The Democratic and Republican parties instead prioritize mobilizing electoral support with appeals to identity, ideology, idealism, and fear. American media coverage and elections are normally pep rallies that obscure present dangers and opportunities. Instead of providing voters with a lucid appreciation of how path-dependent partisan programs are likely to affect them, both parties demonize each other and barrage the public with deceptive idealist appeals. Controlling the narrative is more important to the candidates than candidly addressing present dangers and opportunities. It frees both political parties to stay their respective courses. Their narratives are tales told by idiots full of sound and fury, signifying little.

This volume avoids the media melodrama and refrains from choosing sides. It identifies the power-seeking goals of the Democratic and Republican parties and their path-dependent systemic consequences.

Kamala Harris and Donald Trump offer voters two distinct "existential" futures that only come into focus with detailed examinations of the real present dangers and opportunities.

Key domestic challenges are surveyed in Part IV, while international relations are covered in Part V.

Harris and Trump have not clearly articulated their views on all critical issues. Nonetheless, it is not difficult to assess their rival viewpoints and likely responses to specific present dangers and opportunities.

Part VI considers America's prospects under Harris and Trump regimes. It reveals that the outcome of the November election is likely to matter more fundamentally than most observers appreciate.

A Harris victory will consolidate and expand the elite privileged, anti-competitive, "straitjacket society" that left-wing progressives have constructed over the decades. Entitlement, affirmative action, egalitarianism, and restorative justice programs will determine domestic realities. Underfunded sphere of influence wars abroad will dominate America's international relations.

Progressives are not socialists because workers are not sovereign. Progressivism replaces workers with other "worthy" beneficiaries, supporting elite goals at the expense of the working class.

The "red" revolutionary progressivism that is the foundation stone of Harris's worldview began innocuously enough as a series of welfare policies but morphed into an institutionalized system reminiscent of Cuba's revolutionary socialism that substitutes radical feminists, other sexual orientations, ethnic minorities, and non-whites for the working class. Cuban socialist redness was a wager on egalitarian politics, and blind faith that the nationalization of wealth would magically provide workers with a high quality of existence, when in practice revolutionary socialism camouflaged inequities, depressed living standards, and repressed personal freedom. Left-wing progressivism is having similar consequences in the United States.

It will not fade quietly into the night. Elite activists will fight rather than switch.

Populism reflects the deep disgruntlement of the productive working class in search of an institutionally viable vision and road map. Although witheringly attacked by progressives, Project 2025 marks the start of a process for shaping a sustainable populist movement.[1] A Trump victory will provide populism with the foundation required for the restoration of equal opportunity and traditional values. Defeat will propel the Republican Party in hazy new directions.

Both sides bill the November 2024 American presidential election as "existential." They are right.

---

[1] Project 2025. (2024): Building for conservative victory through policy, personnel, and training. Get the facts. https://www.project2025.org/

The analysis in this volume builds on the following works:

Steven Rosefielde, *Socialist Economic Systems: 21st Century Pathways*, London: Routledge. 2023.

Steven Rosefielde, *Russo-Ukrainian War: Implications for the Asia Pacific*, Singapore: World Scientific, 2023.

Steven Rosefielde and Dan Quinn Mills, *Beleaguered Superpower: America Adrift*, Singapore: World Scientific, 2022.

Contents

About the Authors	v
Preface	vii
Introduction	xiii
Part I Political Theater	**1**
Chapter 1 The Biden–Trump Debate	3
Chapter 2 Party Masks — Real Personalities	7
Part II End Games	**13**
Chapter 3 Closed Society	15
Chapter 4 Open Society	19
Part III Strategic Management	**21**
Chapter 5 Dogma, Semblance, and Power	23
Part IV Domestic Issues	**27**
Chapter 6 A Good Society	29
Chapter 7 The State	35
Chapter 8 Economy	37
Chapter 9 Education	45
Chapter 10 Immigration	49
Chapter 11 Social Discord	55

Part V	Foreign Issues		**59**
Chapter 12	Russo–Ukrainian War		61
Chapter 13	NATO		81
Chapter 14	China		85
Chapter 15	Axis of Iniquity		91
Chapter 16	Hamas–Israeli War		97
Chapter 17	Iran		101
Chapter 18	Cuba		105
Chapter 19	Venezuela		109
Chapter 20	World Order		111
Chapter 21	Entangling Treaties		113

Part VI	Prospects		**115**
Chapter 22	Reckless Endangerment		117
Chapter 23	The Election that could Change the World		119

Conclusion   121

Introduction

American presidential elections for the past 150 years have pitted two establishment parties against each other. Candidates typically are party machine members. Durable machines dispense patronage and other benefits to financial backers under the cover of government contracts and regulatory accommodation. Both Democrats and Republicans claim that their constituents are the "people" but offer distinct programs to best serve constituency needs. The scope and the content of Democratic and Republican programs, driven by electoral competition, are similar. Both support big government, national security, rule of law, law and order, markets, business, full employment, Social Security, public health care, public education, and welfare services financed by deficit spending and ballooning national debt. Both promote democracy, affirmative action, and equal opportunity, restricting electoral competition to platitudes and sloganeering. Both support the North Atlantic Treaty Organization and American global hegemony. Programmatic details matter in diverse ways to special interests but have little bearing on winning presidential elections where Democrats and Republicans prioritize mobilizing electoral support with appeals to identity, ideology, idealism, and fear. American media coverage and elections are normally pep rallies, not scholarly debates. They assiduously avoid debating how to cope best with present domestic and foreign dangers, and fail to provide voters with accurate, full information essential for rational choices. Party machines and their financial backers want to indoctrinate and win, not educate. They and selected constituencies reap the fruits of electoral victory, and beguiled taxpayers pay the bill, assured that the establishment knows its job and does it right.

The 2024 Harris–Trump election is unusually impassioned because Donald Trump is an anti-establishment populist, even though he is running on the Republican ticket. Kamala Harris is a leftist progressive Democratic Party stalwart, but Trump is detached from establishment parties. If elected, Harris can be relied on to continue entrenched domestic and foreign policies with a Democratic Party "Brahmin Left," "closed society" accent,[1] positioning herself as the sword and shield of democracy, entitlements, affirmative action, anti-colonialism, anti-plutocracy,[2] easy access immigration, social justice, and progress. Trump, if elected, will try to alter the entrenched Democratic Party course, downsizing big government, promoting business, and purging progressive modifications of Social Security, public health, education, welfare, and immigration programs. He will strengthen law enforcement, attempt to reduce the national debt, and eradicate "politically correct" suppression of free speech and free thought, including gender taboos and ideological intolerance. In foreign policy, Trump will curb overzealous American hegemony abroad including pro-radical Islamic policies, taking account of the residual influence of the Republican establishment.[3]

Like Harris, Trump perceives himself as the sword and shield of democracy, social justice, and progress, with the caveat that these goals are

---

[1] The term was coined by Thomas Piketty.
Teixeira, R. (2024): A last hurrah for the Brahmin Left? *AEI*. https://www.aei.org/op-eds/a-last-hurrah-for-the-brahmin-left/

[2] Plutocracy means government by the wealthy. Franklin Roosevelt stressed the theme as part of the new deal. Progressives ideologically are anti-plutocratic and anti-capitalist, but are double-minded about collaborating with the rich and famous.

[3] The core of each party is its office holders. Trump is not an office holder, so he is not the center of the party. He became a force in the Republican Party by entering and winning presidential primaries in 2016 and then winning office (the presidency). He is trying to convert the Republicans to his brand of populism, but with limited success. The core of the party is its congresspersons and state office holders, the governors, and state legislators. For the most part, they are not populists. The Republican leadership in the House, including the Speaker (the top Republican office holder in the country) is very competent. They are mostly not populists, even though they support Trump for president. If Trump loses this presidential election, populism may disappear from the party.

The Democrats have many big city mayors and they are very influential in the party. This is not true of the Republicans. The Democrats are much more of an urban party. Mayors take actions, while legislators and even federal executives are much more constrained.

The Democrat identity groups also have spokespersons, some of whom are office holders who are very important in the party.

sought with an "open society" agenda that includes plural viewpoints. He poses a double threat to the establishment. He not only might discard bipartisan establishment policy, his presidency might also drastically reduce financial returns to establishment insiders. Trump is a center-populist, not a Spinozian rational idealist.[4] He is a patriotic, anti-elite politician representing the interests of ordinary disgruntled citizens (the new Workers' Opposition)[5] who receive negligible benefits, are treated with contempt, and forced to pay a large share of the tax bill.[6] He is not a fascist. Harris is more reflexively authoritarian. His rank-and-file supporters are inarticulate.

---

[4] Krauze, E. (2024): A philosopher for our times, *Project Syndicate*. https://www.project-syndicate.org/onpoint/spinoza-free-thought-against-intolerance-illiberalism-by-enrique-krauze-2024-07

[5] The Workers' Opposition was a faction of the Russian Communist Party that emerged in 1920 as a response to the perceived over-bureaucratization that was occurring in Soviet Russia. It was forced to dissolve by the 10th Congress of the Russian Communist Party (Bolsheviks).

[6] Ichabod. (2024): The irrelevance of Biden's senility, *Asia Times*. https://asiatimes.com/2024/07/the-irrelevance-of-bidens-senility/

"Trump speaks truths that no one else who could get a large hearing was willing to speak before 2016. One such truth is that America's ruling elites, abetted by academia, the media and the federal bureaucracy, have impoverished American workers by their ceaseless quest for access to cheap foreign labor through free trade with poor countries and immigration from poor countries. Other such truths are that social justice is not merely or even chiefly a matter of race or gender or sexual preference; that the number of human genders is not infinite; that white skin does not necessarily make one evil; and that keeping Muslims out of the US is a cheaper, more humane and more effective way of protecting America from Islamist violence than is invading Muslim countries."

Kudlow, L. (2024). Give Biden the union elites, while Trump takes the rank-and-file, *Fox Business*. https://www.foxbusiness.com/media/larry-kudlow-give-biden-union-elites-while-trump-takes-rank-file

"Here's what's bothering the Teamsters and the rank-and-file of the other unions as well: Joe Biden has created an affordability crisis for typical working families.

"Their kitchen tables have been squeezed by a 20% rise in overall prices during Biden's term, including a 20% hike in groceries, a near-40% rise in energy, and don't forget gasoline is still $3.50 — compared to just over $2 when Trump left the White House. Looking at the actual numbers, average weekly earnings during Mr. Trump's term rose $5,065 — to $65,216.

"Through May 2024, during Mr. Biden's term, those same weekly earnings declined by $2,968 — really call it $3,000 — to $62,248. In other words, Biden has given working folks a pay cut, whereas Trump gave them a sizeable pay increase.

The left progressive elites (analogous to Weimar Marxists) denigrate them as dystopian "far-right" troglodytes plotting to seize electoral power.

The American establishment and its counterparts abroad could mitigate center-populist threats by reshaping their policies, shifting the tax burden, and sharing the political spoils, but have chosen to double down on their polemics.[7] They are content to demonize Trump and run against what they insist is an emerging fascist menace rather than include populists in the establishment or accommodate their grievances. Progressives substantiate their characterization by stressing that Trump wrongheadedly opposes their "wise" establishment programs and policies. Trump, as the establishment frames the narrative, is malign because he contests progressive legislation, mandates, and judicial decrees. The establishment's mantra, like Stalin's, is *"kto kovo"* (kill or be killed).[8] On July 13, 2024, one Trump opponent took the mantra literally.[9] On September 15, 2024 Ryan Routh attempted to succeed where Thomas Cooks had failed.[10]

The Harris campaign's slogans are stop "weird" Trump, and make Kamala America's first black-Tamil Indian woman president. Trump's populist slogan is empower workers to Make America Great Again!

The first (and only) Biden–Trump debate in June 2024 was an exchange of barbs (sound bites) with little substance. Both called each other liars, crooks, villains, and unguided missiles. The Harris–Trump

---

"Ronald Reagan used to call it take-home pay, and that's been the soft underbelly of the Biden economy for 3.5 years, and that's why he's losing votes among union and nonunion workers."

Teixeira, R. (2024): A last hurrah for the Brahmin Left? *AEI.* https://www.aei.org/op-eds/a-last-hurrah-for-the-brahmin-left/

[7] Teixeira, R. (2024): A last hurrah for the Brahmin Left? *AEI.* https://www.aei.org/op-eds/a-last-hurrah-for-the-brahmin-left/

[8] Conquest, R. (1968): *The Great Terror: Stalin's Purge of the Thirties.* Oxford: Oxford University Press.

[9] Beavers. O and Carney, J. (2024): 'He just won the election': Hill Republicans predict Trump rally shooting will ease path to White House, *Politico.* https://www.politico.com/news/2024/07/13/hill-republicans-trump-rally-shooting-00167995

Hayes, C. (2024): Biden admits Trump 'bullseye' comments a mistake, *BBC.* https://www.bbc.com/news/articles/cd1rzde0n4do

[10] Kayyem, J. (2024): A horrifying new attempt on Trump's life, *The Atlantic.* https://www.theatlantic.com/politics/archive/2024/09/trump-assassination-attempt/679891/

debate in September 2024 was similar. It was staged to "get Trump," leaving the policy fine print vital to America's future unexamined.[11]

This volume addresses the national interest. It identifies the progressive establishment's political trajectory, the populist worker alternative,[12] and parses the opposing visions.

---

[11] The clichés about abortion were especially uninformative.

[12] Dans, P., Chretien, S., and Hemenway, T, (2024): Project 2025. *Heritage Foundation.* https://www.project2025.org/

Trump has wisely distanced himself from Project 2025 to avoid being mired in needless controversy. The Democrats have disregarded Trump disclaimers and aggressively condemned the project.

Sforza, L. (2024): What is Project 2025, Heritage Foundation's outline of conservative priorities? *The Hill.* https://thehill.com/homenews/campaign/4753684-heritage-foundation-project-2025/

"The 2025 Presidential Transition Project is a 900-page 'governing agenda' that details conservative priorities should a Republican win the White House in November. The project's website said it includes the work and insights from more than 400 scholars and policy experts. It's divided into five sections and 30 chapters. The five sections are titled 'Taking the Reins of Government,' 'The Common Defense,' 'The General Welfare,' 'The Economy' and 'Independent Regulatory Agencies.' What are some of the policy proposals? The mandate includes reshaping the powers of the executive branch, gutting small government agencies and removing diversity, equity and inclusion language from federal government. One of the central priorities outlined in Project 2025 includes reimplementing Schedule F, which would reclassify thousands of workers so that they could be subject to swifter firing. The Associated Press noted that this could affect up to 50,000 federal workers. Then-President Trump rolled out an executive order regarding Schedule F in 2020, but President Biden revoked it after he took office. His administration introduced a new rule earlier this year that would make it more difficult for Trump to fire federal workers if he is reelected.

"The handbook also rails against abortion, demanding that the federal government cut funding for abortions in some of its programs and that the Food and Drug Administration (FDA) reverse its approval of abortion pills, such as mifepristone. The foreword states that the next president must 'make the institutions of American civil society hard targets for woke culture warriors.' The foreword said this starts with deleting the terms sexual orientation, gender identity, diversity, equity and inclusion 'out of every federal rule, agency regulation, contract, grant, regulation, and piece of legislation that exists.' It also calls for deleting the terms gender, gender equality, abortion, reproductive health, reproductive rights and 'any other term used to deprive Americans of their First Amendment rights.'"

Part I
Political Theater

Chapter 1

The Biden–Trump Debate

President Joseph Biden and Donald Trump tried to rally supporters and win converts in a traditional pep rally debate broadcast from Atlanta to 51 million viewers on June 27, 2024. Both presidential candidates touted their accomplishments, lambasted their opponent, and tried to bedazzle viewers without meticulously validating their claims and counterclaims. The primary themes addressed were immigration, the economy and inflation, abortion, foreign policy and the wars in Ukraine and Gaza, legal issues of the participants, Social Security, the attack on the United States (US) Capitol on January 6, 2020, and the participants' ages. The themes, given the time constraints, lend themselves to facile, often double-speak responses. Biden and Trump both denied misconduct and denounced each other's duplicity and corruption. They extolled their records on the economy, migration, abortion, and foreign policy, and blamed their opponents for inflation and negative aspects of the wars in Ukraine and Gaza. Biden berated Trump for his callous attitude toward Third World refugees, insinuating racist intent. He chastised him for denying women's right to abortion on demand, even though fathers and the state obviously have legitimate stakes in the issue. Trump chided Biden for being indifferent toward American workers adversely affected by open immigration and his insensitivity to the rights of the "almost" born. The establishment expected that viewers who identified with the concerns of the Democratic Party's target constituencies would laud Biden and loathe Trump. Populist viewers were supposed to do the reverse. It was anticipated that supporters of both sides would be reassured about their leader's competence and the depravity of his opponent, each confident that their hero would carry the day.

The staged political event, however, unexpectedly went off script. Biden was addled, raising the specter that the ravages of age might make him unfit for a second presidential term, and more importantly that the resulting loss of voter support might cost the Democratic Party establishment the election.[1] *The New York Times* sounded the establishment alarm the next day, urging Biden to withdraw his candidacy in favor of a more "bankable" helmsman. Many immediately piled on, creating a raucous political drama where a host of machine and party financial backers jockeyed in their self-interest, ignoring Biden's counter claim that he was competent and the Democratic Party establishment's best choice.

The unseemly episode, which ended in Biden's withdrawal as a presidential candidate on July 21, 2024, has multiple implications.[2] The most

---

[1] Ichabod. (2024): The irrelevance of Biden's senility, *Asia Times*. https://asiatimes.com/2024/07/the-irrelevance-of-bidens-senility/

"Since years before the nationally-televised Biden-Trump debate of June 27, 2024, it has been obvious, to anyone who has paid even a little attention to US public affairs, not only that Biden is increasingly senile but also that his performance of presidential functions has been directed by or through advisors and handlers with deliberately low public profiles."

"If Biden is re-elected, whatever interests are now controlling Biden will continue to control him either through the same advisors and handlers or others of their choosing. That is true regardless of who those advisors and handlers may be. Their identities and specific functions are irrelevant."

Biden's cabinet controls domestic and foreign policy. It includes Vice President Kamala Harris and the heads of the 15 executive departments — the Secretaries of Agriculture, Commerce, Defense, Education, Energy, Health and Human Services, Homeland Security, Housing and Urban Development, Interior, Labor, State, Transportation, Treasury, and Veterans Affairs, and the Attorney General. Additionally, the Cabinet includes the White House Chief of Staff, the US Ambassador to the United Nations, the Director of National Intelligence, and the US Trade Representative, as well as the heads of the Environmental Protection Agency, Office of Management and Budget, Council of Economic Advisers, Office of Science and Technology Policy, and Small Business Administration.

[2] Piper, J. and Fuchs, H. (2024): Kamala Harris takes over war chest as Biden campaign becomes Harris for President, *Politico*. https://www.politico.com/news/2024/07/21/kamala-harris-biden-campaign-funds-00170136. Biden's withdrawal as the Democratic Party's 2024 presidential candidate and his endorsement of Kamala Harris's candidacy did

important non-partisan revelation is that the Democratic Party's paramount priority is preserving establishment power, not leader loyalty and intra-party democracy.[3] Biden received 14 million primary votes (3,896 delegates). He had the right to be the Democratic Party candidate,[4] but backroom power brokers succeeded in pressuring him to withdraw.

American presidential elections are staged to preserve party power by concealing chronic policy failure and crying wolf, not to gauge which candidate is most likely to protect the country, foster prosperity, and advance social justice. Profit-losing companies are forced into bankruptcy in competitive markets, while establishment policies are shielded by a code of silence.

Gauging Harris' and Trump's comparative merits consequently depends not on political theater, but on the path dependence of the two candidates' political management models and program performance. If the programs underperform, competent strategic managers can adopt effective reforms. If the political managers are inflexible, national prospects in an increasingly polarized society are correspondingly dim.

---

not automatically make her the candidate. The candidate in principle should be chosen by primary selected delegates, but can be made by backroom power brokers. Campaign funds for the Biden–Harris campaign can be transferred to Harris, but the Democratic National Committee could also stake a claim. A total of $95 million is up for grabs.

[3] Douthat, R. (2024): There is still a Biden scandal, *The New York Times*. https://www.aei.org/op-eds/https-www-nytimes-com-2024-08-10-opinion-joe-biden-president-html/

"For instance, we learned that Biden hadn't held a full cabinet meeting since last October and that his handlers expected scripted questions from his cabinet officials. We learned that his capacities peak between 10 a.m. and 4 p.m. and diminish outside that six-hour window. We learned that congressional Democrats, liberal donors and some journalists all had exposure to Biden's decline that they didn't discuss publicly until the debacle of the June debate. We learned that none other than Hunter Biden was acting as a close adviser to his father in the crucial days after that debate."

[4] 2024 Democratic Presidential Primary Delegate Tracker Results, August 26, 2024. https://www.usatoday.com/elections/results/2024/democratic/presidential-delegates

Chapter 2

Party Masks — Real Personalities

The Democratic and Republican party machines choose presidential candidates they believe will win elections and implement programs that suit machine purposes. Both use primaries as a device to endear themselves to voters and gauge electability. The contemporary Democratic Party ostensibly binds itself to choose its presidential candidate based on primary-generated delegate counts, but is not legally obligated to do so. Power brokers in the aftermath of Joe Biden's poor debate performance displaced him from the Democratic Party presidential ticket. The Republican Party behaves similarly but permits delegates more latitude.

The character of many presidential candidates consequently is discernible from party agendas and actions, with notable exceptions. Most public personae mirror their party's public face and ulterior motives. Donald Trump is an exception. He has imposed his personality and agenda on an otherwise establishment Republican Party by shifting from a pro-business "laissez-faire" agenda to an inclusionary pro-America populist agenda focused on middle-class workers and family concerns.

Comparison of the Republican Party platforms in 2016 and 2024 spotlights a few key ideological and tactical changes.[1] The main issues are abortion, immigration, education, the economy, and LGBTQ+ rights.

Trump's Republican Party now tolerates early and midterm abortions under state rather than federal supervision. It continues to advocate building a border wall but promises to begin the largest deportation in

---

[1] Sentner, I. (2024): How has Trump transformed the Republican Party? Look at the platforms, *Politico*. https://www.politico.com/interactives/2024/republican-platform-trump-changes/

American history. The 2024 platform promises to defund schools that engage in political indoctrination, specifically instruction about gender, sexuality, and critical race theory, and adopts a "fair trade" rather than "free trade" approach to businesses that slashes regulations, cuts taxes, ensures abundant low-cost energy, and fosters innovation. Finally, the 2024 Republican platform promises to end "left-wing gender insanity" by keeping men out of women's sports, banning taxpayer funding for sex-change surgeries, stopping taxpayer-funded schools from promoting gender transition, reversing Biden's radical rewrite of Title IX education regulations, and restoring protections for women and girls.

Kamala Harris is a left-wing progressive Democratic Party woman. Tim Walz considers her "socialist" on the shallow grounds that "socialism is what some people would call 'neighborliness'."[2] She and her public persona have evolved with the machine's goals and policies. There are two keys to her electoral successes: her moderate persona and affability, and her quick-change artist ability to align her own evolving public positions with those of the party's power brokers. She demonstrated these skills in her September 10, 2024 debate with Trump, where she outshined her opponent.[3] As in the prior Biden-Trump debate, both candidates restricted themselves to bold, facile, often irrelevant claims, and shunned serious analysis.[4]

---

[2] Miller, A. (2024): Potential Harris VP pick ripped for 'weird' socialism comparison to 'neighborliness', *Fox News*. https://www.foxnews.com/politics/potential-harris-vp-pick-ripped-weird-socialism-comparison-neighborliness

[3] Barone, M. (2024): Kamala Harris won the debate, but maybe not the election, *AEI*. https://www.aei.org/op-eds/kamala-harris-won-the-debate-but-maybe-not-the-election/?mkt_tok=NDc1LVBCUS05NzEAAAGVhKYF7R0r7YjUvDbQi6WoTN18BVdPfSg7hFSSupBt_9rPrweMrkCDU0UVxYlkKlWU5KYbl5hSN-mSyNah7hLEKAvZfSfE2_ALYtDsvNwE6hRQlA

[4] The two candidates spent a few minutes debating the abortion issue. Harris reiterated the simplistic pro-choice line that a woman's body should be hers to make decisions. Neither fathers nor the community should be allowed to supervene on any woman's choice. Trump failed to parry Harris' facile claim, saying instead that the decision about the legality of abortion and any qualifications to a woman's right to choose should rest in the decision of each state. Harris gave examples of restrictions on the right to choose which exist in several states and suggested that under Trump those restrictions would spread.

Trump proposed no tax on Social Security benefits and Harris adopted the same position.

Donald Trump, born June 14, 1946, is his own man. The Republican Party or populist machines cannot control him. He has become tactically adept, but otherwise his core goals and policies are unchanged. There are two keys to his electoral successes: his flamboyant, iconoclastic, anti-establishment persona, and aroused disgruntled voters victimized by establishment progressive elites. He graduated from the University of Pennsylvania's prestigious Wharton School with an economics major. Like Biden, Trump received a series of draft deferments and did not serve in the Vietnam War. He has street smarts backed by his father's vast fortune and was a reality television host before entering politics in 2000.

Trump has been consistently pro-"the common man" ("the forgotten men and women of America"), and a "realist" in both his domestic and foreign policy, opposing overzealous progressive gambits. His tent covers all Americans but he rejects aggressive affirmative action, restorative justice and critical race theory. Trump also opposes radical feminist, transgender, pro-abortionist, open immigration and atheistic activism. He does not endorse Foggy Bottom-sponsored color revolutions, transnationalism, Strobe Talbott's global nationalism,[5] radical anti-colonialism, fanatic Islamism, Cuban and Venezuelan socialism, Russophobia, American global hegemony, and nuclear brinkmanship. He is unapologetic for the sins ascribed to him by militant progressives, and can be relied on to stay the course everywhere including Russia and Israel, until objective constraints prevent him from doing so. He is a center populist who will shrink invasive progressive control over the judiciary and bureaucracy, and wasteful public projects that reduce national welfare. He will prioritize equal opportunity over diversity, equity, and inclusion,

---

Harris proposed a substantial increase in the corporate income tax rate. Trump opposed that.

Harris proposed subsidies for first-time home buyers to use for mortgage downpayments, increases in subsidies for rearing children, etc. Trump did not support the idea.

Harris proposed an anti-plutocratic capital gains tax on unrealized capital gains. Trump opposed.

Harris proposed an increase in the capital gains tax rate to the maximum rate on individual income. Trump argued that this would throw the economy into recession.

[5] Talbott, S. (2008): *The Great Experiment: The Story of Ancient Empires, Modern States, and the Quest for a Global Nation*, New York: Simon and Schuster.

defunding racial and gender employment preferences[6] and the bloated administration and propaganda programs supporting them. This will not only eliminate unfairness, but will reduce inferior service. He will rescind radical government environmental, business, and social regulations. Trump will drastically decrease immigration for those falsely claiming refugee status, and defund excessive refugee welfare support.[7] He will try to restore Social Security to its original purpose as a retirement insurance program for FICA (Federal Insurance Contributions Act) taxpayers, eliminating free riders. Trump will try to undo Biden's $400 billion student loan forgiveness giveaway funded by tomorrow's taxpayers.[8] Trump will try to rationalize federal healthcare by ensuring that medical insurance payers have access to the services they need without being pauperized by the system's vagaries. He will build on the Supreme Court's decision to overturn *Roe v. Wade*. Trump will promote equitable free trade, competitive business, accelerated economic growth, full employment, low inflation, and federal debt reduction by streamlining regulation and tax cuts in lieu of "industrial policy." While rejecting industrial policy (government subsidization of selected companies and business activities), Trump favors American reindustrialization, especially in the military industrial subsector.

His foreign priorities are equally clear. He will extricate America from the Ukrainian morass,[9] and protect Israel from Hamas' plot to expel Jews from the Middle East. Trump will improve relations with Saudi Arabia to deter Houthi and Iranian aggression, support Cuban and Venezuelan democratization, and substitute diplomacy for gray zone sphere of influence and proxy wars. He will avoid transnational

---

[6] Calder, R. (2024): The 'woke' ways of President Biden and Kimberly Cheatle's US Secret Service, *New York Post*. https://nypost.com/2024/07/20/us-news/the-woke-ways-of-kimberly-cheatles-us-secret-service/

[7] Camarota, S. (2024): The Cost of Illegal Immigration, *National Affairs*. https://nationalaffairs.com/publications/detail/the-cost-of-illegal-immigration

[8] Brickman, M. (2024): Checking in on the Biden Administration's Higher Education Regulatory Agenda, *AEI*. https://www.aei.org/education/checking-in-on-the-biden-administrations-higher-education-regulatory-agenda/

[9] Vance, J. (2024): The math on Ukraine doesn't add up, *The New York Times*. https://www.nytimes.com/2024/04/12/opinion/jd-vance-ukraine.html

entanglements like the Trans-Pacific Partnership, Paris Agreement on climate change, and flawed Iranian nuclear non-proliferation agreements. The platform argues for a strong military used sparingly and, even then, only in national interest.

Trump cannot build a united America with militant progressives, but can accommodate moderate members of the Democratic Party.

Part II
End Games

Chapter 3

Closed Society

The Democratic Party was created as a vehicle to elect Andrew Jackson in 1828. It supported strong presidential power, geographic expansionism, progressive policies, and opposed imperialism. Pro- and anti-slavery factions divided the Democratic Party in the pre-Civil War era. Democrats championed the protection of private property and personal wealth, while opposing extreme income and wealth inequality.

After Franklin D. Roosevelt (FDR) became president in 1932, the Democratic Party promoted a progressive platform that included support for Social Security and unemployment insurance. It was isolationist and opposed immigration during the 1930s. After World War II, the Democratic Party discarded isolationism and embraced the role of free world protector, duty-bound to remake people everywhere in the Western elite's image. Domestically, the Democratic Party distanced itself from the working class in the 1960s (but not large trade unions), promoted non-European immigration, and adopted an increasingly militant entitlement, affirmative action, and a restorative justice agenda, privileging and transferring income and power from the middle class to Blacks, minorities, immigrants, elite feminists, and transgender activists.

The Democratic Party is not wedded to a monolithic ideology. Power brokers adjust platforms to obtain and preserve political power, making them responsive to demographic trends and zeitgeist shifts. In the 21st century, the party is strongest among urban voters, union workers, college graduates, youth, women, African Americans, immigrants (legal and illegal), sexual minorities, and the unmarried. On social and economic issues, it advocates for entitlement, equal opportunity, affirmative action, restorative justice, anti-meritocracy, civil law enforcement indulgent to criminals, high immigration quotas, open refugee access, abortion rights, the legalization of marijuana, sexual license, and LGBTQ+ rights, while paying lip service to egalitarianism (Gini coefficients remain stubbornly high).[1] Progressives are hostile to traditional family and religious values (except Islam) and plutocratic business, with some ideological exceptions. In foreign policy, the Democratic Party supports the West's global hegemony over Russia, China, and the Global South, as well as sphere of influence expanding "color revolutions." Segments of the party sympathize with Marxist–Leninist Cuba and Venezuela, and anti-colonialist Third World activism. The Democratic foreign policy establishment is conflicted over Israel, Palestine, Iran, Saudi Arabia, and Iraq. Cold War legacy Democrats prioritize American hegemony. Radical Democrats champion anti-colonialism, the Palestinian cause, and Third World socialism. The Democratic Party throughout the Cold War actively promoted arms control and disarmament. Barack Obama committed America "to seek the peace and security of a world without nuclear weapons,"[2] but these concerns faded as the Biden administration gradually accepted the risks of winning the Russo–Ukrainian proxy war.[3]

The Democratic Party's policy preferences are important, but only tell half of the story. Its power brokers are addicted to micro-managing individuals and society, cowing opposition, and transferring income and power to their "deserving." They disregard the grave economic and social harm inflicted on most Americans by left-wing progressive zealotry.

The Democratic Party is a hodgepodge of incompatible interest groups with a unitary veneer committed to defeating Trump and populism. Elderly and other moderate voters are encouraged to believe in the FDR tradition that the Democratic Party stands for the inclusive, anti-totalitarian, democratic, patriotic, anti-militarist, peaceful, just, and compassionate welfare state. They support socially inclusive and tolerant consensus

---

[1] This statement refers to Gini coefficients computed before taxes and transfers. The adjusted figure yields a lower Gini coefficient without a marked trend.

Early, J. (2018): Reassessing the facts about inequality, poverty, and redistribution, *CATO*. https://www.cato.org/policy-analysis/reassessing-facts-about-inequality-poverty-redistribution

[2] Pifer, S. (2019): 10 years after Obama's nuclear-free vision, the US and Russia head in the opposite direction, *Brookings*. https://www.brookings.edu/articles/10-years-after-obamas-nuclear-free-vision-the-us-and-russia-head-in-the-opposite-direction/

[3] Postol, T. (2024): Biden's 'new' nuclear strategy and the super-fuse that sets it off, *Responsible Statecraft*. https://responsiblestatecraft.org/biden-nuclear-strategy/

building to achieve national harmony. They applaud equal opportunity and appreciate the need for moderate affirmative action, but are unenthusiastic about transgressive anti-meritocratic, racial, minority, elite feminist, and transgender initiatives designed to build electoral majorities. They are chary of military adventurism and are inclined toward arms control and disarmament. This base is moderate in domestic and foreign affairs.

Party power brokers in the new millennium, however, have chosen to prioritize militant courses at home and abroad. Left-wing progressives have carried the day in social programs. Hawks dominate foreign policy. This is the Democratic Party's "closed society" endgame: progressive control at home and hawkish global hegemony abroad. Opposition is punished and repressed. The mission is "closed" because although tolerant "open society" options are available that allow rival groups to accommodate each other, zealous progressives continuously escalate their demands and impose their will on the unwilling. The Soviet Union, Pol Pot's Cambodia, Cuba, and Venezuela illustrate the despotic concept. America's Democratic Party progressives adhere to Lenin's authoritarian style of securing political power in the name of the oppressed, substituting minorities, elite women, and non-traditional sexual activists for the working class. This is why they are not socialists. A system that exploits workers for the benefit of elites cannot be socialist.

The Democratic Party's closed society paradigm is systematized and hardwired, and will persist until the power brokers determine that its coercive domestic agenda and high-cost global hegemony policy no longer constitute a winning electoral formula.

Double-thinking and double-speaking Democratic Party power brokers have successfully managed to conceal the drastic divide between the party's moderate base and militant domestic and foreign policy wings from public scrutiny. Nonetheless, the divide is important because it exposes the vulnerability of the Democratic Party's grip on national power. American youth is growing increasing disaffected,[4] and domestic and foreign policy militants may soon target each other instead of populism.

---

[4] Abrams, S. (2024): Shocking number of young Americans no longer believe in the American Dream, *Fox News*. https://www.aei.org/op-eds/shocking-number-of-young-americans-no-longer-believe-in-the-american-dream/

Chapter 4

Open Society

The Republican Party is a hodgepodge of competing interests. It was committed to libertarianism, free trade, big business, and opposed to trade unions until Donald Trump re-oriented it to defending workers against China's "beggar thy neighbor" protectionist trade policies and thwarting Democratic Party closed society policies, including unrestricted immigration.[1] He is even trying to woo the International Brotherhood of Teamsters, traditionally anchored to the Democratic Party, into his populist fold.[2]

Donald Trump is not a philosopher, but conducts himself in accordance with Karl Popper's "open society" concept.[3] He rejects progressive claims that Marxism scientifically proves that repressing the liberty of

---

[1] The Democratic Party hopes that open immigration will permanently inure its political control, creating a de facto closed society one-party system. Mason, M. (2024): How Trump and Republicans 'won the war' on immigration, *Politico*. https://www.politico.com/news/2024/07/16/trump-republicans-immigration-00168838

"'Before we were talking about a pathway to citizenship for 35 million people' said Felipe Benitez, a Latino political strategist and immigration advocate. 'Now we're barely figuring out if we can get 500,000 spouses of U.S. citizens protected status.'

"Trump has said immigrants are 'poisoning the blood of our country.' And if he wins again, a centerpiece of his agenda is a plan to deport up to 20 million people, using the military if necessary."

[2] Gonyea, D. (2024): Teamsters President Sean O'Brien addresses the Republican National Convention, *NPR*. https://www.npr.org/2024/07/16/nx-s1-5041345/teamsters-president-sean-obrien-addresses-the-republican-national-convention

[3] Popper, K. (1945): *The Open Society and its Enemies*, London: Routledge.

opponents generates superior outcomes.[4] He dismisses the progressive claim that the virtue of its policies requires everyone to obey them. Instead, Trump embraces a tolerant open society alternative that requires rivals to accommodate one another enough to mitigate civil strife. Trump has softened his stance against homosexual marriage, abortion, and egalitarianism. He is willing to make modest concessions on affirmative action, but remains unwilling to accommodate progressive demands for entitlement and restorative justice. Of course, he has no objection to progressives charitably supporting their various causes on their own dime.

Trump supports downsizing the federal bureaucracy, rationalizing Social Security, unemployment insurance, and welfare for people unable to fend for themselves. In foreign policy, Trump intends to negotiate a peace settlement with Russia, but is open to diverse sources of advice about terms. There are exceptions to his open society credentials. His plan to deport 25 million illegal immigrants offers a heavy-handed resolution to a complex problem, but for the most part his outlook is compatible with the Democratic Party's moderate base. Trump's open society future is a light welfare state buttressed by entrepreneurial *élan*,[5] free competition, fair trade, and expansive civil liberties (but not licentiousness), low taxes, and a substantially reduced bureaucratic burden. Trump intends for the Republican Party to remain nationalist, populist, and "America First" for generations to come. Traditional Republicans are becoming increasingly sympathetic with Trump's concept of a worker-friendly, fair, and free enterprise.[6] But few high-profile senior Republican Party statespersons are endorsing his presidential candidacy.[7]

---

[4] Rosefielde, S. (2023): *Socialist Economic Systems: 21st Century Pathways*, New York: Routledge.

[5] Varadarajan, T. (2024): J. D. Vance and the Indian-American Dream, *Wall Street Journal*. https://www.wsj.com/articles/j-d-vance-and-the-indian-american-dream-2024-election-usha-81ddedd0

[6] Hubbard, G. (2024): The economic populists have a point, *Wall Street Journal*. https://www.wsj.com/articles/the-economic-populists-have-a-point-vance-trump-growth-trade-ae9457e8

[7] Goldberg, J. (2024): This is the problem with former Republican Rep. Liz Cheney's endorsement of Kamala Harris. *AEI*. https://www.aei.org/op-eds/this-is-the-problem-with-former-republican-rep-liz-cheneys-endorsement-of-kamala-harris/?mkt_tok=NDc1LVBCUS05NzEAAAGVhKYF7XJIQ62ZQ2ae88v-8AFsEt3zcOXVZ7-mgEu-xEHGqrmwyYtrbJYG7mX8ilniI67TmCK9P1jQT92xwTHRr5Tcg1_vzKiiED-bcLBzW3LjJg

Part III
Strategic Management

Chapter 5

Dogma, Semblance, and Power

The Democratic and Republican party establishments and Trump populists claim that their programs will yield wonderful results. The claims are dogma — strongly believed non-evident propositions that adherents refuse to discuss rationally (Pyrrhonism).[1] Progressives insist that entitlement, affirmative action, equal opportunity, restorative justice, and anti-meritocracy will maximize America's quality of existence. Donald Trump counterclaims that terminating most of these programs will increase the quality of American existence.

True believers of either persuasion can try to maximize America's quality of existence by conjuring methods to precisely calibrate social utility and maximize it.[2] The goal is achievable in theory, but impossible in practice. The effort will carry true believers of both persuasions in a totalitarian direction, because, as everyone should have figured out by now from the Soviet experiment, human behavior is disharmonious. If one

---

[1] Pyrrhonism is an Ancient Greek school of philosophical skepticism which rejects dogma and advocates for the suspension of judgment over the truth of all beliefs. It was founded by Aenesidemus in the first century BCE, and said to have been inspired by the teachings of Pyrrho and Timon of Phlius in the fourth century BCE.

[2] Hoffer, E. (1951): *The True Believer: Thoughts on the Nature of Mass Movements*, New York: Harper and Brothers.

Bergson, A. (1938): A Reformulation of Certain Aspects of Welfare Economics, *The Quarterly Journal of Economics*, Vol. 52, No. 1, 310–334.

Rosefielde, S. (2023): *Socialist Economic Systems: 21st Century Pathways*, New York: Routledge.

insists on an exclusive concept of perfection, the government must micromanage everything.³ Dissent for true believers is heresy.

Neither the establishment nor Trump insists on perfection. The illusory semblance of perfection suffices, shaping strategic management and policy. For Democratic Party moderates, the semblance of perfection is lauding Franklin D. Roosevelt's (FDR's) welfare state legacy, holding the line against retreat, and claiming the future by reforming and expanding the welfare state. The approach is simple and effective if the electorate acquiesces. The Democratic Party must merely praise itself, promise more of the same, placate disgruntled factions with extra public spending, and parry external criticism by blaming others for adverse outcomes. The strategy's principal risks are internal and external calls for radical change and entropy. Progressives contend that fine-tuning is insufficient, and demand that the Democratic Party chart a better course. Moderates tolerate suffocating red tape, waste, fraud, and inefficiency in public programs by ignoring the problem.

The progressive political management strategy is narrower, reflecting the left elite's contemporary priorities in entitlement, affirmative action, egalitarianism, restorative justice, and anti-meritocracy. The semblance of perfection for Democratic Party progressives is billeting and featherbedding the bureaucracy, judiciary, Congress, Senate, presidency, and non-governmental institutions including private business and universities with dogma-approved personnel, complemented with dramatic increases in deficit-financed public spending on progressive projects and/or repurposing established welfare state programs. Progressives also demand anti-competitive restrictions on big businesses, accompanied by large equality creating income and wealth taxes on the affluent, and stakeholder control of private companies,⁴ unconcerned about adverse productivity effects. Although they promise prosperity, equality for them

---

[3] Totalitarianism is a political system and a form of government that prohibits opposition political parties, disregards and outlaws the political claims of individual and group opposition to the state, and controls the public sphere and the private sphere of society. Arendt, H. (1951): *Origins of Totalitarianism*, New York: Schocken.

[4] Rosefielde, S. (2020): Progressive Capitalism in a Radical Age, *Journal of ASEAN PLUS+ Studies*, Vol. 1, No. 1, 29–34.

Rosefielde, S. (2021): Stakeholder Capitalism: Progressive Dream or Nightmare? *HOLISTICA — Journal of Business and Public Administration*. https://doi.org/10.18662/lumproc/gekos2020/03

Stiglitz, J. (2019). *People, Power, and Profits: Progressive Capitalism for an Age of Discontent*, New York: W.W.Norton.

is more important than the standard of living. They are willing to accept high inflation and flagging economic growth, together with significant declines in national living standards and the quality of existence, if they can claim token success. The semblance of success is good enough, supported with statistics on billeting (appointment quotas), stakeholder statistics, Gini coefficients, and public spending. The path of least resistance in the contemporary Democratic Party progressive scheme leads in the direction of a progressive version of revolutionary Cuban and Venezuelan pauper socialism.[5] This is bliss for many progressives, but Democratic Party moderates are unlikely to concur. FDR welfare state proponents may find themselves unexpectedly preferring Trump populism after suffering the reality of elite progressivism.[6]

Trump's political management strategy mirrors the moderate Democratic Party approach, with important differences. His populist semblance of success is paring and rationalizing existing institutions and purging radical progressive entitlement, affirmative action, egalitarian, and restorative justice programs. His reforms will increase personal freedom for most Americans. Moderate Democrats will welcome Trump's advocacy of fair trade, worker protection, and reduced foreign entanglements, but this agenda will irk both Democratic and Republican establishment proponents of free trade and American global hegemony. Despite the calumny against Trump, the semblance of success criteria embraced by populists will support a convergence of both parties to a pre-World War II common moderate base. Populists will continue to prefer more liberty to social engineering and Democratic Party moderates will be inclined in the opposite direction, but there will be ample space for consensus building. The conflict between Trump populists and Democratic Party moderates is less than meets the eye. Radical progressivism is the root of America's political polarization.

---

[5]Rosefielde, S. (2023): *Socialist Economic Systems: 21st Century Pathways*, New York: Routledge. Chapter 10 (Castroism).
[6]Rosefielde, S. (2023): *Socialist Economic Systems: 21st Century Pathways*. New York: Routledge. Chapter 20 (Egalitarian Socialism).

Part IV
Domestic Issues

Chapter 6

A Good Society

Ideology

Progressives and populists hold conflicting views of a good society. Neither has a sacred text (like Karl Marx and Friedrich Engels' *The Communist Manifesto*). Their credo is discernible from their rhetoric, identities, heroes, villains, missions, and attitudes toward each other. Progressives perceive themselves as righteous "supermen" for a just society that compensates and privileges oppressed races, ethnicities, women, sexual outcasts, and anyone else with grievances against traditional Judeo-Christian culture. They consider Donald Trump a gauche, reactionary demagogue in league with neocolonialists determined to return Blacks, minorities, and women to servitude, depriving them of their hard-won freedom.[1] They view tolerance and consensus as impediments to defending gains and completing their revolution.

Trump populists perceive themselves as defenders of all productive citizens adversely affected by progressive intolerance, primarily in America but also across the globe. The elite, from their perspective, are parasitic. They live off workers' surplus value. Most populists do not want to roll back the clock to a traditional golden age. They accept change and diversity, but simply reject being victims of progressive priorities.

Progressive and populist attitudes are dogmatic, and hence ideological, because their concepts are articles of faith. They view each other

---

[1] Phillips, S. (2024): *How We Win the Civil War: Securing a Multiracial Democracy and Ending White Supremacy for Good*, New York: New Press.

through a prism of stereotypic ideals that serve their purposes and care less than they claim about real human well-being. Progressives do not prove that traditional enmities bar competitive minority assimilation. Anti-traditional elites simply assert that justice delayed is justice denied. Trump populists do not dispassionately weigh progressive arguments for diversity, equity, and inclusion. They insist that the harm inflicted on the nation is unwarranted.

The gap between the two positions can be bridged with critical reason and stepwise accommodation (consensus building), but neither side shows any interest in doing so.

Moral Dissonance

Progressives and populists hold diametrically opposed views of ideal moral conduct. This is a corollary of progressive anti-traditionalism (including the Judeo-Christian tradition) that impairs a search for common ground. Traditionalists adhere to the Ten Commandments. They deem lust, promiscuity, abortion, adultery, sodomy, homosexuality, immodesty, pandering, and other forms of iconoclasm that threaten family and community integrity sinful. Progressives scoff and embrace a counter agenda destigmatizing traditionalist misbehavior, flouting puritanism, and proselytizing the principle that if it feels good, then it is good for you. Traditionalists occasionally sin, and progressives sermonize, but the lapses do not establish fertile common ground. Both dogmas find their opponents repugnant.

Global Nation versus Make America Great Again

Nationalism and patriotism are traditional values that support an exclusionary order. Progressives wave the flag when it suits their purposes (rallying the electorate against Russia), but are inclined toward anti-colonialist internationalism that liberates everyone from patriarchal shackles. They preach the gospel of universal liberation and Strobe Talbott's global nation.[2] Trump and his populist followers champion Make America Great Again patriotism.

---

[2] Talbott, S. (2008): *The Great Experiment: The Story of Ancient Empires, Modern States, and the Quest for a Global Nation*, New York: Simon and Schuster.

Quality of Existence

Progressives and populists promise prosperity, but they are more concerned about building the good society of their dreams. Both would prefer to live under their respective ideological regimes than switch sides for a few dollars. The quality of existence is a composite measure of utility from all sources, including both material consumption (per capita gross domestic product) and other intangible benefits like democracy, equality, cooperation, freedom, religion, and social justice. Kamala Harris and Trump are both confident that the quality of existence for the constituencies that matter to them will be infinitely higher under their reigns.

Race

The progressive vision of a good society turns on racial, gender, and minority social justice. Race is primary. It had been a central focus in American politics during the slavery period, and thereafter through the Civil War, Reconstruction, civil rights movement, and restorative justice periods.

Abraham Lincoln was a Republican. He freed America's slaves in 1863, and the Southern Democrats were responsible for Jim Crow laws in the late 19th and 20th centuries.[3] Although civil rights were not included formally in Franklin D. Roosevelt's (FDR's) New Deal, Roosevelt's wife Eleanor was a staunch advocate, gradually leading the Democratic Party toward promoting racial integration. Lyndon Baines Johnson grabbed the baton in 1965, advancing the concept of affirmative action and shifting the Democratic Party's race policy from equal opportunity in the direction of affirmative action, entitlement and restorative justice. This included the use of quotas, mandates, and social transfers to foster after-tax income equality and elevate the social status of the Blacks. The Republican Party rejects restorative justice, but supports modest affirmative action and entitlement programs. Currently, 83% of Black voters are Democrats or

---

[3] The Jim Crow laws were state and local laws introduced in the Southern United States in the late 19th and early 20th centuries that enforced racial segregation, "Jim Crow" being a pejorative term for an African American. Such laws remained in force until 1965. Formal and informal racial segregation policies were present in other areas of the United States as well, even as several states outside the South had banned discrimination in public accommodations and voting.

lean Democratic, while 12% align with the Republican Party. They constitute 14% of eligible voters, and most will vote for Kamala Harris.

Hispanic and Asian Voters

Hispanic and Asian voters lean toward the Democratic Party, but with signs of some reversal during the 2024 campaign. Currently, 65% of Hispanic and Asian voters are Democrats or lean Democratic, while 35% align with the Republican Party.[4] They constitute 14% of eligible voters, and most will vote for Kamala Harris.

Feminism

The Democratic Party in the new millennium has positioned itself for electoral purposes as feminism's champion. It seeks to attract women aggrieved by various aspects of their lives. Rapid cultural, ethical, educational, economic, social, and technological changes have altered gender opportunities and obligations, creating both excitement and distress. Moderate and progressive Democratic Party officials astutely promise government action to expand options for women and mitigate their discontents.[5] Radical feminists who reject traditional lifestyles receive plaudits for their audacity. Moderate women receive commiseration, legal reform, and social assistance.

The Democratic Party demonstrates its sincerity with entitlement and affirmative action tactics, such as making high-profile political appointments, spotlighting female candidates, mandating quotas in the private sector, denouncing "glass ceilings," and pressing for wage equality

---

[4] Gramlich, J. (2020): What the 2020 electorate looks like by party, race and ethnicity, age, education and religion, *Pew Research Center*. https://www.pewresearch.org/short-reads/2020/10/26/what-the-2020-electorate-looks-like-by-party-race-and-ethnicity-age-education-and-religion/

[5] Abrams, S. and Kotkin, J. (2024): Will we survive the sex war? *UnHerd*. https://unherd.com/2024/08/will-we-survive-the-sex-war/

"The future, it seems, will belong to those largely disconnected individuals who somehow find a way to negotiate what the US Surgeon General has described as an epidemic of loneliness. Already by 2020, 28% of all occupied homes in the US were one-person households, up from just 8% in 1940. Three years later, Pew found that 10% of Americans had no close friends."

regardless of merit. It hopes to parley these initiatives into a winning presidential strategy. Hillary Clinton was the first test case. She failed, but Kamala Harris now is carrying the baton.

The Republican Party establishment is slowly recognizing the need to attune programs to the changing concerns of modern women, but has not fully risen to the challenge because of its continuing high regard for traditional family values and its distaste for varieties of progressive libertinism. It can and should devise a competitive moderate feminist agenda. Donald Trump's working-class constituency may be even more adverse to moderate and radical feminist change than the Republican establishment.

Feminism is probably the Democratic Party's principal advantage, if it can resist belittling traditional family values.

Deviancy

The Democratic Party also champions non-feminist deviancy from traditional family values for electoral purposes. The acronym LGBTQIA+ (lesbian, gay, bisexual, transgender, queer or questioning, intersex, asexual, and more) covers most of the terrain. It seeks to attract all LGBTQIA+ individuals who look toward the government to facilitate their assimilation into legitimate society and provide affirmative action pathways for a higher quality existence. The group does not have viable alternatives in the Republican establishment and Trump's populist faction. It is an electoral plus for the Democrats.

Chapter 7

The State

The Democratic Party beginning with Franklin D. Roosevelt (FDR) has consistently favored a larger and more centralized government than Republicans. The Democrats' preference for a large federal government is a corollary of their desire to substitute the state for private services. They prefer central administration because this allows progressives to impose their policies on states and municipalities under Republican control. It is safe to infer that the federal government will grow and expand its tentacles under a Kamala Harris presidency, and it may do so too if Donald Trump wins, but at a slower pace. Trump may say that small is beautiful and will pare progressive programs, but these efforts could be offset by countervailing increases in government support for populist constituencies.

The American state is primarily in the "transfer" business. The largest transfers are Social Security and Medicare. Worker and business FICA (Federal Insurance Contributions Act) and Medicare taxes fund current and future payments back to qualified participants. Government bureaucracies set rules and execute the transfers. The cost of rule setting and processing is included as government services (income) in gross domestic product. Other tax revenues are outsourced to politically chosen private businesses providing services to government and private recipients. Government welfare programs check eligibility and transfer money to qualified applicants. States receive tax revenues from federal authorities on a revenue-sharing basis. The Department of Defense is the primary exception. It, too, is preoccupied with transfers and outsourcers, but payments to military and administrative personnel have few private sector counterparts.

The principal driver of government size is its transfer and regulatory programs. Federal and state governments featherbed bureaucracies, and administrators meddle rather than co-manage with principals. Downsizing can mitigate these efficiency problems and related waste, fraud, and abuse. Politics (politocracy), rather than efficiency and social merit, sustains the system, making rationalization difficult in an environment where political advantage takes precedence over the quality of the people's existence.[1]

Court Packing

President Joe Biden's attempt at packing the Supreme Court to the Democratic Party's advantage (endorsed by Harris) provides a vivid example of how partisan political power takes priority over national welfare. The Biden administration sent Congress a proposal to remove conservative Supreme Court judges by imposing term limits on their positions and holding them accountable for "ethical violations" (disagreeing with progressives).[2] Legal scholars have rejected his arguments for decades.[3] Biden himself had agreed in 2023, but recently changed his mind, claiming that conservative supreme court judges' attitudes were "not normal."[4] Although he is a lawyer, the president offered no judicial explanation for his change of heart. Minimal government is apt to be better than a system where big government politicians conflate expediency with national welfare.

---

[1] See Rosefielde, S. and Mills, Q. (2013): *Democracy and its Elected Enemies: American Political Capture and Economic Decline*. New York: Cambridge University Press.

[2] Nazzaro, M. (2024): Bill Barr: Biden's reforms would purge Supreme Court's conservative justices, *The Hill*. https://thehill.com/regulation/court-battles/4798492-bill-barr-biden-supreme-court-reform/

[3] White, A. (2024): Don't repackage court-packing, *AEI*. https://www.aei.org/op-eds/dont-repackage-court-packing/

[4] Cancryn, A. (2024): Biden will blast Supreme Court as 'not normal' as he endorses term limits, binding ethics rules, *Politico*. https://www.politico.com/news/2024/07/29/biden-supreme-court-reform-announcement-00171594

Chapter 8

Economy

Markets and government forces shape American economic performance.

America's markets are imperfectly competitive, allowing large oligopolistic firms to earn excess profits. The state regulates the economy with macroeconomic monetary and fiscal policy, taxation (including graduated income taxes), subsidies, Social Security, Medicare, unemployment programs, social transfers, antitrust laws and mandates. If America were perfectly competitive, per capita gross domestic product (GDP) would increase. The price of anti-competitiveness and government misregulation is deadweight efficiency loss. It is enormous.

The precise magnitude and incidence of the deadweight efficiency loss varies from administration to administration. The policy debate among progressives, moderates, and populists affects America's sustainable economic growth rates, other macroeconomic variables (inflation and employment), the magnitude of anti-competitive state programs, income transfers, non-monetary rationing (quotas), and a host of non-monetary economic benefits (costs), income inequality, environmental degradation, immigration, congestion, liberty, and democracy.[1]

---

[1] It is possible in principle to calibrate individual utilities and sums across individuals. But the task is impractical. Also, as economists often forget, ethical judgments are independent of utility, adding a further intractable aspect to the problem of measuring social welfare objectively. See Bergson, A. (1938): A Reformulation of Certain Aspects of Welfare Economics, *Quarterly Journal of Economics*. Vol. 52, No. 1, 310–334. Individuals can sense whether they are better or worse off today than yesterday, but persuasive composite measures do not exist.

America's core new millennium economic story is simple. Aggregate economic performance has been positive, but per capita GDP growth (living standard) has been subpar despite vigorous entrepreneurship. Labor force participation rates have been low.[2] Unemployment rates (except for the global financial crisis in 2008–2009 and the Covid episode in 2020–2021) have been low.[3] Real wage growth has been low.[4] There have been bouts of inflation (including hidden inflation) and crises. Interest rates (subsidizing consumption and investment, and penalizing savers, especially retirees) have been extraordinarily low. There has been a vast expansion of state transfers and regulation. Billionaires have benefited from high-income inequality.[5]

The net result of these trends is politically charged. The expansion of state programs (mostly diversity, equity, and inclusion related programs) and inept government management between 2008 and 2023 cost the nation at least $6 trillion in foregone GDP,[6] compounded by immense non-monetary utilitarian losses from forced substitution and job quotas (rationing).

The beneficiaries of expansionary monetary policy and transfers gained. The middle class bore the burden of foregone GDP, with many finding themselves substantially worse off in 2024 than in 2008. Progressives justify the skew as "anti-neoliberalism."

---

[2] The labor force participation rates in 2000, 2008, and 2020 were 67, 60, 62, respectively.

Bradley, C., White, O., and Mischke, J. (2024): America's productivity growth is recovering to pre-great financial crisis rates. Europe has more work to do, *McKinsey Global Institute*. https://www.mckinsey.com/mgi/overview/in-the-news/americas-productivity-growth-is-recovering-to-pre-great-financial-crisis-rates

[3] American economic growth has been declining in the new millennium. The long-run historical growth from 1820 to 2000 was approximately 3.3%. It fell after the Global Financial Crisis of 2008 to 2.5%.

[4] Kotlikoff, L. (2024): Harris needs new ideas — here are ten. https://larrykotlikoff.substack.com/p/harris-needs-new-ideas-here-are-ten

"Median real weekly earnings are just 10 percent higher than they were a half century ago."

[5] Median marginal net tax rates facing high-earners are already close to 60%. Billionaires are an entirely different story. They are paying little to no taxes and are generally doing so through entirely legal means.

[6] Real per capita GDP growth declined in the new millennium. The decline was most pronounced after the 2008 financial crisis and has continued falling after the Covid-19 epidemic. It is currently 2% per annum compared with the long-term average of 3.2% per annum.

The standard macroeconomic stories about per capita GDP growth, full employment, low inflation, and national debt are irrelevant to winners and losers except for electioneering purposes. Progressives gladly sacrifice trillions in GDP for the transfer gains achieved by their favored recipients (including themselves). They would tolerate zero per capita GDP growth, as is the case in much of the European Union unless stagnation imperiled their hold on power.

Populists bearing the deadweight loss burden are aggrieved. They will remain so even if the cost of egalitarianism and anti-meritocracy were less.

Progressives will vote for Harris. Populists will vote for Trump.

If Harris wins the November election, future asymmetric gains and losses will intensify. Per capita GDP growth will asymptotically approach zero as it did in the Soviet Union,[7] and transfers will further diminish working-class welfare.[8] If Trump wins, the skew will shift in the opposite direction.

Progressives ascribe the $6 trillion foregone GDP growth loss to slower technological advancements/innovations. This is possible because the attribution of growth to various sources is an art more than a science. Nonetheless, American technological change appears brisker than the aggregate statistics suggest, and the negative effect of diversity, equity, and inclusion masked in employment statistics is consistent with workplace grumbling.

Stealthy Egalitarianism

Many progressives believe that the good society should provide everyone with an equal and secure income. Although they avoid making egalitarianism a priority campaign issue, Democratic Party progressives stealthily strive to achieve the goal with a myriad of transfers including Biden's student loan forgiveness initiative. Some understand that this goal necessarily depresses effort, productivity, entrepreneurship, and technological progress.[9] If leaders prioritize egalitarianism over productivity, there must be a deadweight loss. Living standards must lie below competitive potential. The same principle

---

[7]Rosefielde, S. (2007): *The Russian Economy: From Lenin to Putin*. New York: Wiley.
[8]Aris, B. (2024): Escalating trade war and the West's falling competitiveness. https://bneeditor.substack.com/p/escalating-trade-war-and-the-wests
[9]Rosefielde, S. (2023): *Socialist Economic Systems: 21st Century Pathways*. New York: Routledge, Chapter 20 (Egalitarian Socialism). This inference assumes that at least one person is not altruistic.

holds for economic growth and development. If egalitarianism causes America to lose its competitive edge in the international market, rival entrepreneurial nations will capture lucrative US businesses for themselves, further diminishing the standard of living. American living standards are not fated to decline because technology-driven productivity growth can lift all boats. Nonetheless, anti-egalitarian rival nations may displace American supply chains, and rapidly develop and outstrip the West. Systems matter. If American progressives want to simultaneously wage war against the East and pursue egalitarian and anti-meritocratic economic ends, they may discover that the US economy cannot achieve both objectives.[10]

Band Aids

Both Harris and Trump have failed to articulate the skews embedded in their economic programs. They focus instead on promising sops to their constituencies. Harris promises price controls on food,[11] subsidies to first-time homebuyers, and higher business taxation, including taxing unrealized corporate capital gains (affecting mutual fund dividends to all shareholders). Trump promises to abolish tax on Social Security. Their proposals are band aids, not serious suggestions for improving America's quality of existence.

Social Security, Welfare, and National Debt

Social Security, welfare, and America's national debt need urgent attention. The problem is looming insolvency. The Social Security program will soon lack the cash to pay pledged benefits. Means-tested social-welfare spending totaled $1.6 trillion in 2023.[12]

---

[10] Some counterargue that egalitarianism fosters growth stimulating creativity. It has not done so in the European Union in 2008–2024.

[11] Mills, D. (1969). *Government, Labor and Inflation: Wage Stabilization in the United States*, Chicago: University of Chicago Press.

[12] Gramm, P. and Arrington, J. (2024): Welfare is what's eating the budget, *Wall Street Journal*. https://welfare-is-whats-eating-the-budget.tiiny.co/?mkt_tok=NDc1LVBCUS05 NzEAAAGVicxcr1-besJO3D20EfM9QGydILGBupQS1_oIeaoPRtq2zeMri-JG-bsMCmOzpmkbzL4DcaaqnL7zOkNcQxNnmqClQ4EFogK3C3ALdJCD8pLHCQ

"Since funding for the War on Poverty ramped up in 1967, welfare payments received by the average work-age household in the bottom quintile of income recipients has risen

Politicians may have to choose between cutting programs to reduce the national debt or defaulting on government securities ("haircuts"). Progressives and Trump are disinterested in both problems.[13] Progressives and populists blithely kick the can down the road. Voters should care, especially about defaults on a portion of the national debt, because this raises the specter of a global financial crisis, but most prefer to disregard the danger.

Defense

America's military industrial defense sector requires drastic adjustment.[14] Washington designed the system for global power projection in the wake of World War II. The Pentagon expected to fight wars abroad with large volumes of high-tech weapons. The North Atlantic Treaty Organization and other allies purchased and maintained a substantial portion of weapons produced in America.

This made the United States the "arsenal of democracy," stocked with sufficient weapons to meet existing deterrent needs. America today, however, manufactures weapons in small batches at high unit cost, foregoing learning curve high-volume cost savings. It ended the draft in 1971, increasing personnel costs (wages plus mandated social expenditures), compounded by affirmative action, environmental, and drug enforcement expenses. The upshot of these changes is that Russia and China can project hard power in their primary theaters of military operation at a small fraction of America's cost and have a deeper prolonged war military-industrial capability.

---

from $7,352 in inflation-adjusted 2022 dollars to $64,700 in 2022, the last year with available household income data. This 780% increase was 9.2 times the rise in income earned by the average American household."

[13] Pomerleau, K. (2024): Social Security benefits should not be tax free, *AEI*. https://www.aei.org/economics/social-security-benefits-should-not-be-tax-free/

Federal debt held by the public (not monetized by the Fed) is now 97% of GDP, heading to 166% of GDP by the mid-century. The deficit captures only those obligations Congress puts on the books. Take Social Security's off-the-books, and the deficit becomes a long-term $63 trillion unfunded liability. That is not 97%, but 217% of this year's GDP!

[14] Federal defense spending as a share of GDP is at a post-war low, whereas global threats are at a post-war high.

The Democratic and Republican party establishments are talking as if they are prepared to fight the Russo–Ukrainian War, China in the Asia-Pacific, and Iran in the Middle East for as long as it takes without grasping that they cannot afford to do this without radically adjusting America's military industrial system, and transferring resources from social programs to defense. Trump populists and most American voters likewise are benighted. The issue receives negligible attention from either political party.

Ecology

Ecology is a major global challenge. There are 8.1 billion people today living on the planet, a figure forecast to reach 10 billion by 2050. Humans consume vast amounts of non-renewable resources, risk depleting energy reserves, pollute the environment, and may be adversely affecting climate change. Voters of all persuasions recognize the potential benefits of public ecological regulation and welcome constructive action, but attitudes vary widely about what should be done. Dogmatists are convinced that the sky is falling. They claim that unless the government undertakes monumentally expensive actions to end the use of fossil fuels, ban gasoline-powered cars, and build alternative infrastructure, the result will be catastrophic. United States Treasury Secretary Janet Yellen, for example, claimed that the global transition to a low-carbon economy will require $78 trillion ($3 trillion in new capital each year through 2050).[15] She framed this as the biggest economic opportunity of the 21st century, but neglected to consider who would pay the bill. If ecological investment is increased, other social expenditures must contract. There are no free lunches.

The evidence supporting the dogmatist position is shaky and often specious,[16] but is treated as Gospel by true believers.

Activist antics repel skeptics who prefer a gradualist, learning by doing approach, but cannot prove that their counter policies are ideal.

---

[15] Yellen, J. (2024): Yellen says $3 trillion needed annually for climate financing, far more than current level, *Yahoo Finance*. https://finance.yahoo.com/news/yellen-says-3-trillion-needed-190251232.html

[16] Pielke Jr., R. (2024): We don't need no stinking science, *AEI*. https://www.aei.org/articles/we-dont-need-no-stinking-science/

"Neglecting to address climate change and the loss of nature and biodiversity is not just bad environmental policy. It is bad economic policy."

The issue is polarizing voters. The progressive wing of the Democratic Party believes that championing the climate crisis theme is a significant plus for their candidates. Moderates are perplexed, and populists who will suffer most from hasty climate crisis programs will vote with Trump for a balanced approach.

Global Taxation

Progressives at home and abroad favor a world government that makes American taxpayers fund foreign progressive projects. They advocate for "anti-neoliberal hyper globalization."[17] United Nations activists are leading the charge, as they did for similar reasons with the Paris Agreement.[18] Harris' record suggests that she would support the United Nations initiative. Trump would adamantly oppose it.

Tax Free Social Security

Trump has suggested eliminating tax on Social Security.[19] Seniors, especially workers who defer retirement (while receiving Social Security

---

[17] Hassan, D. (2024): The contribution of wealth: How tax justice can deliver global public goods, *Carnegie Endowment for International Peace*. https://carnegieendowment.org/research/2024/08/the-contribution-of-wealth-how-tax-justice-can-deliver-global-public-goods?lang=en

Sagasti, F. (2024): An international financial transactions tax for international public goods, *Carnegie Endowment for International Peace*. https://carnegieendowment.org/research/2024/08/an-international-financial-transactions-tax-for-international-public-goods?lang=en

[18] The Paris Agreement is an international treaty on climate change that was signed in 2016. The treaty covers climate change mitigation, adaptation, and finance. The Paris Agreement was negotiated by 196 parties at the 2015 United Nations Climate Change Conference near Paris, France. As of February 2023, 195 members of the United Nations Framework Convention on Climate Change (UNFCCC) are parties to the agreement. Of the three UNFCCC member states which have not ratified the agreement, the only major emitter is Iran. The United States withdrew from the agreement in 2020, but rejoined in 2021. The agreement recognizes the rights of parties to use emissions reductions outside of their own borders toward their Nationally Determined Contributions, in a system of carbon accounting and trading. Activists have tried to use the mechanism as a device for America financing less developed countries, but the effect has been negligible.

[19] US Budget Watch 2024. (2024): Donald Trump's suggestion to end taxation of Social Security benefits, *Committee for a Responsible Federal Budget*. https://www.crfb.org/blogs/donald-trumps-suggestion-end-taxation-social-security-benefits

benefits), will welcome Trump's initiative because they lack adequate savings. Their ranks are rapidly swelling because real living costs substantially exceed published statistics. Investment advisors are now counseling the working class to remain in the labor force to avoid poverty.

The rationale for the tax is that workers (but not the self-employed) do not pay tax on the employer contribution to FICA (Federal Insurance Contributions Act) and therefore should pay tax on deferred benefits. The argument is logical, but not binding because self-employed Social Security recipients do pay full FICA tax (they are double taxed under the present system) and Congress has the power on a compassionate basis to make Social Security payments tax-free. The taxation of Social Security benefits today reflects progressive priorities that Trump does not share. His suggestion is pro-populist.

Progressives and many moderates legitimately note that if Social Security benefits are tax-free, then Social Security must receive funding from other sources or benefits cuts.[20] The objection is not fatal. Joe Biden's student loan forgiveness scheme will cost $1.4 trillion in foregone revenue, nearly enough to cover the shortfall from tax-free Social Security benefits. The problem posed by terminating tax on Social Security payments is just an aspect of the budget deficit and national debt problem that politicians someday will be forced to resolve.

---

[20] Tax on Social Security benefits is earmarked for the Social Security retirement trust fund. For seniors earning a combined income above $34,000 per year ($44,000 for married couples), an additional 35% of benefits are taxable, with this revenue going toward the Medicare hospital insurance trust fund.

US Budget Watch 2024. (2024): Donald Trump's suggestion to end taxation of Social Security benefits, *Committee for a Responsible Federal Budget*. https://www.crfb.org/blogs/donald-trumps-suggestion-end-taxation-social-security-benefits

The article estimates that making Social Security benefits tax- free will:

- "Increase deficits by $1.6 trillion to $1.8 trillion through 2035
- Increase Social Security's 75-year shortfall by 25 percent — or 0.9 percent of payroll
- Nearly triple the Medicare HI 75-year shortfall, increasing it by 0.6 percent of payroll
- Advance the insolvency date of Social Security's retirement trust fund by over one year
- Advance the insolvency date of the Medicare HI trust fund by six years"

Chapter 9

Education

The annual Best Countries Report, conducted by US News and World Report, BAV Group, and the Wharton School of the University of Pennsylvania, reserves an entire section for education.[1] The report surveys thousands of people across 78 countries, then ranks these countries based on the survey's responses. The education portion of the survey compiles scores from three equally weighted attributes: a well-developed public education system, would consider attending university there, and provides top-quality education. The United States ranked first in 2023.

The assessment is surreal. According to a Business Insider report in 2018, the United States ranked 38th in math scores and 24th in science, implying that America's educational performance in other disciplines compensates for poor showing in math and science. The impact of diversity, equity, and inclusion (DEI), together with critical race theory and anti-meritocratic and anti-colonialist indoctrination, makes American education seem best.

Reality is just the reverse. Progressive educational dogma, skyrocketing class size, absenteeism, overburdened teachers, the purge of politically incorrect faculty and disciplines (Classics), the explosion of corrupt academic research, artificial intelligence-assisted cheating, anti-meritocratic grading, infotainment, and administrative featherbedding have transformed America's educational institutions into DEI indoctrination centers for the enrichment of elite administrators and the benefit of the

---

[1] Education Rankings by Country 2024, *World Population Review*. https://worldpopulationreview.com/country-rankings/education-rankings-by-country

Democratic Party. The system swindles students. They waste their time with busy work, agonizing about guilt, worrying about sexual identity, and chasing rainbows at the expense of basic skills and critical thinking. Dogma has become the new knowledge.

Testing is absurd. Professors cannot gauge students' comprehension of core principles because they have too many exams to grade, and their graduate assistants cannot do the job fairly. Instructors are compelled to write perfunctory true or false questions, reward students for other skills, and allow them to grade themselves with the result that grades and recommendation letters have no objective meaning. Grade inflation is rife.

DEI and the larger progressive agenda supporting them including critical race theory lie at the root of the problem and will not vanish any time soon despite the Supreme Court ruling banning DEI. Universities are already notifying their communities that they can simulate compliance.[2]

The heart and soul of the Biden administration's special contribution to American education is "student loan" forgiveness.[3] Joe Biden has already forgiven more than $400 billion, primarily by extending the Covid-19 payment pause. The overwhelming share of his efforts are very likely illegal.

The initiative is both a vote-buying ploy and a devious attempt to create free universal and progressive higher education for individuals at high taxpayer cost, a burden that inevitably falls on the shoulders of the middle class because the poor do not pay taxes and the rich find ways to evade.

President Biden's top higher education priority is granting and forgiving as many loans as possible. So far, his administration has proven effective at doing so. The Supreme Court struck down Biden's marquee loan forgiveness policy, but his education policy agenda suggests that he will try again before the election. The most consequential program is SAVE

---

[2] University Communications (2024): UNC System shares guidance regarding DEI, The University of North Carolina at Chapel Hill. https://www.unc.edu/posts/2024/07/15/unc-system-shares-guidance-regarding-dei/

"The revised Board of Governors' policy calls for a detailed look at the diversity and inclusion initiatives on UNC System campuses, ensuring that University efforts do not infringe on academic freedom, equal opportunity or institutional neutrality."

[3] Brickman, M. (2024): Checking in on the Biden Administration's Higher Education Regulatory Agenda, *AEI*. https://www.aei.org/education/checking-in-on-the-biden-administrations-higher-education-regulatory-agenda/

(Saving on a Valuable Education Plan), which incentivizes millions to borrow as much as possible for their education as well as living expenses with the expectation that much of it will be forgiven. As of now, SAVE is partially paused by multiple courts, with higher courts likely to weigh in. In the long-term, SAVE would spell disaster for multiple parties in higher education, propping up the most expensive college programs with the worst labor market outcomes and encouraging students to borrow more, colleges to raise prices, and colleges that currently avoid issuing loans to begin doing so. Increased community college borrowing could allow millions of Americans to put their living expenses on the government's tab and never pay it back.[4]

The administration is not finished. Regulatory filings indicate a separate planned October "surprise" to create hundreds of billions more in mass loan forgiveness despite the Supreme Court making clear that the Department of Education has no such power. Undaunted, Secretary Miguel Cardona insisted that "federal courts have issued rulings in lawsuits brought by Republican elected officials who are siding with special interests and trying to block Americans from accessing all the benefits of the most affordable student loan repayment plan in history."[5] He continued, "Let me be clear: President Biden and I are determined to lower costs for student loan borrowers ... no matter how many times Republican elected officials try to stop us," before concluding with a promise: "We'll keep fighting for you!" For Biden this seems to require "packing" the Supreme Court.[6]

The Democratic Party is content to accept the US and World Report accolade that America's educational system is number 1. Harris will throw more good money after bad into expanding the progressive educational establishment and programs. They will stick in their thumb and pull out a

---

[4]Brickman, M. (2024): Can Biden expect a final Supreme Court showdown on student loans? *AEI*. https://www.aei.org/education/can-biden-expect-a-final-supreme-court-showdown-on-student-loans/

[5]Brickman, M. (2024): Can Biden Expect a Final Supreme Court Showdown on Student Loans? *AEI*. https://www.aei.org/education/can-biden-expect-a-final-supreme-court-showdown-on-student-loans/

[6]Nazzaro, M. (2024): Bill Barr: Biden's reforms would purge Supreme Court's conservative justices, *The Hill*. https://thehill.com/regulation/court-battles/4798492-bill-barr-biden-supreme-court-reform/

plum, saying what a good boy they are. The country will take one step further toward imitating revolutionary socialist Cuba.

Trump populists oppose everything that is wrong with contemporary American education. Donald Trump will press the Department of Education to purge progressive educational distortions and return to the basics.

The electoral impact of education issues on voters is sensitive to cohort and ethnic groups. It is likely to be very significant for parents in the age bracket of 20–50, Blacks, and minorities. Trump will probably be the primary beneficiary, but students hoping for debt forgiveness and those attracted to DEI and critical race theory doubtlessly will vote for Harris.

Chapter 10

Immigration

Immigration is an emotionally charged issue for progressives, populists, and moderates. Radical progressives advocate granting all foreigners unrestricted access to America, bountiful welfare support, voting privileges, and on-demand citizenship. They insist that the benefits of open access outweigh the costs. Trump populists counterclaim that costs exceed benefits and advocate expelling illegal immigrants. Moderates hold mixed views. The problem is complex because immigrants are heterogeneous, their motives differ, and they diversely affect citizens (in terms of employment, wages, income, as well as tax burden, and cause environmental, sociological, political, and psychological distress). The United States admits immigrants legally and uses a quota system based on nationality, skills, wealth, and political status to determine access. The government treats most seeking access as economic immigrants. They are subject to quotas, but refugees (victims of war and persecution) are granted exceptions. Children born in the United States to foreigners are automatically citizens, providing a special pathway for their parents and relatives to join them. American attitudes toward immigration vacillate. Immigration has occurred in waves, with periods of high and low quotas, favoring different ethnic groups. Race and religion at times have been decisive factors. The immigration wave that began under Lyndon B. Johnson had prioritized non-Europeans and significantly diminished the share of Whites in America's population. Economic and social impacts also affect immigration. Businesses view immigrants both as a source of cheap labor and high skill talent. They strongly advocate for increased immigration to reduce domestic skill shortages. Trade unions and independent workers prefer low quotas to protect their jobs and wages. Sundry minorities lobby for increased quotas and special refugee access on behalf of their brethren. Immigration activists argue that it boosts employment and gross domestic product (GDP). Political parties keep a sharp eye on expected electoral impacts, and all factors are interdependent.

The current wave of immigration is provocative because of its extraordinary size, adverse worker impact, high net social cost, and political ramifications. President Joe Biden and the progressive wing of the Democratic Party aggressively pressed for increased immigration quotas, fast-tracked refugee access, encouraged mass illegal immigration (lax border enforcement and sanctuary cities), and increased public expenditures to support the influx. Although data on illegal economic and refugee migrants are inherently suspect and must be adjusted for illegal migrant emigration, the big picture shows a tidal wave of Biden administration-encouraged net immigrant inflows attributable jointly to increased legal quotas and illegal immigrants. The net benefit of this influx (income generated and taxes paid, less welfare support) has been negative, but tolerable for advocates. The full economic burden is greater when non-welfare public services such as educational expenses required to teach non-English speaking students are included, but even these costs are the tip of the iceberg. Various segments of the population perceive other disutilities not counted in GDP and public spending statistics as immense. These costs include pressure on workers and middle-class housing (public and private), education (including diversity, equality, and inclusiveness), medical access, transportation, congestion, crime, terrorism, and political strife. Professional assessments of immigration costs and benefits concentrate on GDP, public expenditures, and employment statistics, ignoring other utilities. The narrow focus prevents a lucid appreciation of immigration's emotional charge. Progressives, populists, and moderates are pleased when the statistics support their positions and disregard them when they do not. What really matters for them are electoral politics, ideals, and outrage. Open immigration progressives and closed immigration populists vehemently oppose each other, making immigration a key presidential campaign battleground.

The Biden Immigration Wave

No one disputes the surge in immigration encouraged by the Biden administration, but the precise number is heatedly debated. The correct order of magnitude appears to lie in the vicinity of 2.7 million. The Biden immigration surge is not a figment of fevered populist imagination. Census

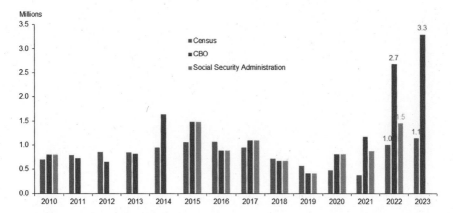

Figure 10.1. CBO estimates of net immigration far higher than Census, Social Security Administration in 2022, 2023

Notes: Net international migration. Census change is from July 1 of the previous year to July 1 of the given year.
Sources: U.S. Census Bureau; Congressional Budget Office (CBO); Social Security Administration. Federal Reserve Bank of Dallas.

2023 estimates (July to July) put net immigration at 1.1 million, far from the Congressional Budget Office's (CBO) calendar year 2023 estimate of 3.3 million (Figure 10.1). CBO similarly estimated a much higher net immigration number than other agencies in 2022 — 2.7 million.[1]

Net immigration is the sum of individuals who enter the country minus those who leave. Entries can be permanent or temporary but exclude short-term visitors such as tourists. Entries can also be legal, when people come with United States government visas, or otherwise, such as humanitarian migrants.

The CBO included real-time data that cast doubt on the lower immigration estimates in Figure 10.1.

Border surge sets record

Customs and Border Protection (CBP) personnel encountered 2.54 million migrants at the southwest border in 2023 alone (Figure 10.2). This is

---

[1] Orrenius, P., Pranger, A., Zavodny, M., and Dhillon, I. (2024): Unprecedented U.S. immigration surge boosts job growth, output, *Federal Reserve Bank of Dallas*. https://www.dallasfed.org/research/economics/2024/0702

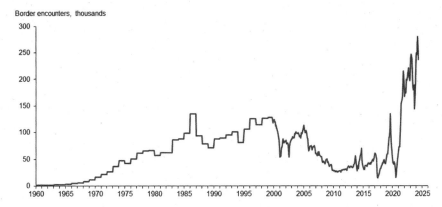

Figure 10.2: Migrant encounters on southwest border rise to record levels post-pandemic

Notes: Data are through April 2024. Data before October 1999 are only available at the annual level; those figures are the annual fiscal year numbers divided by 12. Monthly figures are seasonally adjusted.

Sources: Customs and Border Protection; seasonal adjustments by the Federal Reserve Bank of Dallas.

about the same as the 2.58 million migrants in 2022, a record year. The pre-pandemic annual average was 500,000 migrants.

Since the pandemic began in the US in February 2020, CBP has recorded almost 8 million encounters at the southwest border. Steven Camarota clarifies the phenomenon,[2] stressing the astonishing magnitude of illegal immigration. All told, during the first three years of the Biden administration, 6 to 7 million new illegal immigrants likely settled in the United States. The figure is unprecedented.

Camarota believes that the main reason so many people started showing up at the border at the end of 2020 was Biden's campaign promise to get rid of Trump-era immigration policies. The Biden administration also contributed to the problem by ending agreements with several Central American countries that curtailed illegal migration.

The Biden immigration wave has greatly increased the immigrant share of America's population. There are now 51.6 million immigrants,

---

[2] Camarota, S. (2024): The cost of illegal immigration, *National Affairs*. https://nationalaffairs.com/publications/detail/the-cost-of-illegal-immigration

legal and illegal together, living in the United States. This is a new record. Immigrants today make up 15.6% of the U.S. population — more than triple what it was in 1970. This surpasses the old records of 14.8% in 1890. America has entered terra incognita.

The enormous strain on social services immigrants are creating in cities across the country suggests that many are arriving with few resources and skills. Camarota also points out that in the first part of 2024, 41% of all immigrants ages 18 to 64 who came to the United States during the prior two years reported they had at least a college education. As recently as 2018, it was 53% for all new arrivals.

The Net Economic Cost of Immigration

Although the issue is controversial, Camarota's careful parsing of the evidence illuminates the cause and net economic cost of all categories of immigration into the United States. He finds that illegal immigrants are almost certainly a net fiscal drain.[3]

The reason is that a very large share of illegal immigrants are inadequately educated which results in modest incomes and tax payments. This enables many of them to qualify for means-tested welfare programs, which they often receive on behalf of native-born children. Illegal immigrants are a net fiscal drain on public budgets. They receive more in benefits from the system than they pay into it.[4]

As the 2024 presidential election neared, the Biden administration, recognizing its vulnerability on the immigration issue, passed an executive order to shut down the border if illegal crossings reached an average of 2,500 migrants a day in a given week, or roughly 875,000 per year. The order suspended protection for asylum seekers without a "credible fear" for requiring asylum, allowing for immediate deportation of unauthorized migrants.

---

[3] Camarota, S. (2024): The cost of illegal immigration, *National Affairs*. https://nationalaffairs.com/publications/detail/the-cost-of-illegal-immigration

[4] Camarota, S. (2024): The cost of illegal immigration, *National Affairs*. https://nationalaffairs.com/publications/detail/the-cost-of-illegal-immigration

Harris has not articulated how she intends to solve the immigration crisis. Commentators infer them to suit their purposes.[5] Given her progressive credentials, she is apt to doublespeak and foster another immigration wave should she become president. Trump promises to reduce all forms of immigration drastically, including ending birthright citizenship to the children of non-citizens.[6]

---

[5] Hogen, M. (2024): Trump vs. Harris on immigration: Future policy proposals, *Peterson Institute for International Economics*. https://www.piie.com/blogs/realtime-economics/2024/trump-vs-harris-immigration-future-policy-proposals

[6] For a full list of Trump's anti-immigration program see Hogen, M. (2024): Trump vs. Harris on immigration: Future policy proposals, *Peterson Institute for International Economics*. https://www.piie.com/blogs/realtime-economics/2024/trump-vs-harris-immigration-future-policy-proposals

Chapter 11

Social Discord

Defund the Police

Law and order is a sleeper issue in the 2024 presidential election. Statistics show an uptick in violent crimes and a decline in other categories after 2020. There is no consensus explanation for these trends. Progressives, moderates, and populists all oppose crime in principle, with various qualifications. Progressives attribute high big city criminal activity and high African-American incarceration rates to racism and poverty; others offer little comment. They also correctly note that immigrants exhibit low crime rates.

Crime rates can affect elections in swing states and localities, but usually become a critical factor when linked to accusations of systemic racism and poverty. Progressives have not forgotten the issue and make racism a central battle cry, but no longer ardently demand defunding police.

Progressive activists pushed for police defunding in the wake of riots and demonstrations triggered by the death of George Floyd at the hands of the Minneapolis police in 2020. Derek Chauvin, the officer responsible, was convicted of murder and sentenced to 22 and a half years in prison.

The defund movement has gained substantial momentum. A small minority of the progressive lawmakers within the Democratic Party, including Ilhan Omar, Rashida Tlaib, and Alexandria Ocasio-Cortez, support defunding the police, believing that "policing in our country is inherently and intentionally racist." They have called for police departments to be dismantled, but have also provoked a backlash that encouraged Democrats to subsequently downplay the issue.

Trump, sensing the new mood, tweeted "The Radical Left Democrats new theme is 'Defund the Police". Remember that when you don't want Crime, especially against you and your family. This is where Sleepy Joe is being dragged by the socialists. I am the complete opposite, more money for Law Enforcement!"[1]

In the 2020 elections, Republicans running in competitive districts successfully flipped many Democratic-held seats by associating the Democratic candidate with the slogan "defund the police." Both Democrats and Republicans have cited association with the defunding movement as a contributing factor in the Democrats' loss of seats in the 2020 House elections and the poorer-than-expected results in other Democratic campaigns.

Trump will try to inject the theme in the 2024 presidential election.

Abortion

The United States abortion-rights movement (also known as the pro-choice movement) is a sociopolitical action initiative supporting the proposition that a woman should have the legal right to an elective abortion, meaning the right to terminate her pregnancy. It is part of a broader global abortion-rights campaign. The movement consists of a variety of organizations, with no single centralized decision-making body. Kamala Harris endorsed the position in her debate with Donald Trump on September 10, 2024.

Abortion is a divisive moral and political issue. It affects the entire community, men and women alike. The nub of the matter is termination. Should women be compelled to carry pregnancies through to birth, or do they have the right to abort?

The issue is moral because opponents of the movement consider abortion a mortal sin, while advocates prioritize their will over the sanctity of life. It is political because governments have the power to regulate the behavior of everyone under their jurisdiction. American women do not have the political right to commit suicide or engage in prostitution even though some insist that they alone are entitled to control their bodies. Nor

---

[1] https://x.com/realDonaldTrump/status/1268635752214208514

can they categorically claim that fathers should not have stakeholder rights.

Progressives in the Democratic Party staunchly support women's exclusive right to abort with few restrictions. Populists, especially those with strong religious convictions, adamantly oppose elective termination.

Partisans on either side of the issue cannot prove to adversaries that their positions are superior. There are some grounds for compromise. Trump tries to sidestep alienating his anti-abortion supporters by leaving decisions to state authorities. He appears to have alienated some supporters, but pro-life voters have no alternatives and will probably cast their ballots for Trump. Harris has not plumbed the middle ground, and advocates for full "reproductive freedom."[2] She champions the restoration of *Roe v. Wade*.

Moderates in both parties favor diverse compromises, including limits on late term abortions. Populists in 2020 were ardently anti-abortion, but in the aftermath of *Dobbs v. Jackson Women's Health Organization* that overturned *Roe v. Wade*, the Trump 2024 campaign has been content to leave the issue to state authorities.

Some believe that the issue of abortion will decide the November presidential election in Harris's favor. They may be right.

---

[2] Messerly, M. and Ollstein, A. (2024): Kamala Harris' call for 'reproductive freedom' means restoring Roe, *Politico*. https://www.politico.com/news/2024/07/29/kamala-harris-abortion-restoring-roe-00171657

Part V
Foreign Issues

Chapter 12

Russo–Ukrainian War

The Russo–Ukrainian War could be a decisive issue in November, subject to battlefield and/or diplomatic surprises. Its impact is unpredictable. Donald Trump will garner many anti-war voters. Those who accept the Biden administration narrative will vote for Kamala Harris, accepting the allegation that Trump is Moscow's pawn.

The war has a complex history, but the responsibility lies mainly with the Biden administration. It began with Russian forces invading Ukraine on February 24, 2022, occupying and selectively annexing territory. Russian troops were quickly driven from the outskirts of Kyiv, and later retreated to the east bank of the Dnieper River, but seized a large slice of the Black Sea Coast including a land bridge to Crimea.[1] The battle seesawed thereafter with Russia expanding its control by fighting a war of attrition.

---

[1] For war maps, see Ukraine in maps: Tracking the war with Russia, *BBC*. https://www.bbc.com/news/world-europe-60506682

The causes and implications of these events are murky and contested.[2] The conflict's roots are disputable and obscured by James Jesus Angleton's "wilderness of mirrors."[3]

The Biden administration attributed the war to Russia's "unprovoked" aggression, seeking to restore Kremlin control over former Soviet imperial space.[4] Russia was cast as Goliath; Ukraine as David.

Vladimir Putin denies invading Ukraine, counter-claiming that the Kremlin deployed an "expeditionary force" (special military operation) to eradicate neo-Nazi partisans,[5] and protect Russian citizens in Luhansk,

---

[2] Motivation analysis is tautological. At best, premise-based inferences are tested with ambiguous patterns. Ludwig Wittgenstein called this inferential process tautological because inference merely follows from premises.

Wittgenstein, L. (1922): *Tractatus Logico-Philosophicus*, London: Kegan Paul.

Simon, H. (1957): A Behavioral Model of Rational Choice, in Simon (ed.), (Simon, 1990) *Models of Man: Social and Rational-Mathematical Essays on Rational Human Behavior in a Social Setting,* New York: Wiley.

Kahneman (2003). Maps of Bounded Rationality: Psychology for Behavioral Economics, *The American Economic Review*, Vol. 93, No. 5, 1449–1475.

[3] Historical justification cannot resolve the Russo–Ukrainian War. The more ancient the claims, the less bearing they have on negotiated solutions in the absence of military victory.

Martin, D. (1981): *Wilderness of Mirrors: Intrigue, Deception, and the Secrets that Destroyed Two of the Cold War's Most Important Agents*, New York: Harper Collins.

[4] The primary evidence for this contention is Putin's repeated claim that Novorossiya (most of contemporary Ukraine) belongs historically to Russia, backed by the Kremlin's military modernization drive from 2010 to 2015 and annual large-scale war games conducted from 2015 to 2021. Putin's decision to limit the scope of the 2014 Ukraine occupation by contrast illustrates Russia's restraint.

Karatnycky, A. (2024): Russia is back to the Stalinist future, *Foreign Policy*. https://foreignpolicy.com/2024/03/24/russia-putin-stalin-soviet-election-war-repression-political-prisoners/

[5] Ripp, A. (2022): Ukraine's Nazi problem is real, even if Putin's 'denazification' claim isn't, *NBC News*. https://www.nbcnews.com/think/opinion/ukraine-has-nazi-problem-vladimir-putin-s-denazification-claim-war-ncna1290946

Donetsk, and Crimea. He blames Western intervention in Ukraine for Moscow's subsequent escalation.[6]

Putin contends further that Russia neither declared war on nor attacked the North Atlantic Treaty Organization (NATO) (Ukraine is not a NATO member), and that the Kremlin is not at war with it.

NATO concurs. It refrained from deploying troops in Ukraine to repel Russia, precisely because this would constitute an act of war, choosing instead to provide Kyiv with lethal, technical, and financial assistance.

Although, these facts and principles do not preclude escalation (bending "red lines"),[7] the legal nuances helped contain the conflict (including

---

[6] "Dmitry Peskov asserted the Russia's actions in Ukraine remain and special military operation and do not legally constitute a war, despite escalation."

Korybko, A. (2024): Analyzing the Kremlin spokesman's unprecedented description of the Ukrainian conflict as a war. https://korybko.substack.com/p/analyzing-the-kremlin-spokesmans

"Peskov's unprecedented description of the Ukrainian conflict as a 'war' should therefore be seen as the Kremlin's clearest signal yet that it'll respond to the scenario of a conventional Western intervention by striking those opposing forces in line with the international laws governing this form of conflict. The reason behind publicly conveying this intent is to prompt France and the other states like the UK, Poland, and the Baltic States that might also be contemplating a conventional intervention to rethink their plans."

RT. (2024): Russia is at war — Kremlin. What started as a military operation has escalated after the West became a participant, Dmitry Peskov has said. https://www.rt.com/russia/594669-ukraine-war-russia-kremlin/

[7] France and Lithuania contingently advocate direct intervention.

Porter, T. (2024): A NATO country says it could join Ukraine's war with Russia if 2 conditions are met, *Business Insider*. https://www.businessinsider.com/nato-emmanual-macron-france-join-ukraine-war-on-russia-conditions-2024-5

Macron said he would consider sending French troops to Ukraine "if the Russians were to break through the front lines, if there were a Ukrainian request, which is not the case today."

Yemets, M. and Mazurenko, A. (2024): Macron doesn't rule out sending troops to Ukraine if Russians break through line of contact, *Ukrainska Pravda*. https://www.pravda.com.ua/eng/news/2024/05/2/7453964/

the use of tactical nuclear weapons)[8] in the absence of international proxy war statute.[9]

Mediation or arbitration of the Russo–Ukraine proxy war are possible, but NATO and Russia have shunned both options, preferring to muster public support, mobilize resources, and fight, rather than redress grievances through diplomacy, legal process, or other non-violent means.[10] Both

---

Intellinews. (2024): Lithuanian leaders back sending 29,000 military-age men back to Ukraine. https://www.intellinews.com/lithuanian-leaders-back-sending-29-000-military-age-men-back-to-ukraine-323441/

[8] The term "proxy war" covers a broad range of armed conflicts in which principals use agents of avoid formal declaration of war between principals (Berman, E. and Lake D. A. (2019): *Proxy Wars: Suppressing Violence through Local Agents*, New York: Cornell University Press; Groh, T. L. (2019): *Proxy War: The Least Bad Option*, California: Stanford University Press.). The West has steadily bent the redlines defining its Ukrainian proxy war. John Helmer outlines the ideas of Russian defense experts for retaliating in a danger escalation game.

Luttwak, E. (2016): *The Grand Strategy of the Roman Empire: From the First Century CE to the Third*, Baltimore: John Hopkins University Press.

Luttwak, E. (1993): *The Endangered American Dream: How to Stop the United States from Becoming a Third World Country and How to Win the Geo-economic Struggle for Industrial Supremacy*, New York: Simon & Schuster.

Luttwak, E. (2024): It's time to send Nato troops to Ukraine: After 75 years, the alliance is locked in the nuclear age, *Unherd*. https://unherd.com/2024/04/its-time-to-send-nato-troops-to-ukraine/

Cimbala, S. and Korb, L. (2024): Putin's nuclear warnings: Heightened risk or revolving door? *Bulletin of Atomic Scientists*. https://thebulletin.org/2024/03/putins-nuclear-warnings-heightened-risk-or-revolving-door/

Helmer, J. (2024): Next stage — the General Staff's targets after Putin's feint. https://johnhelmer.net/next-stage-the-general-staffs-targets-after-putins-feint/print/

Sachs, J. (2024): Why won't the US help negotiate a peaceful end to the war in Ukraine? *Common Dreams*. https://www.commondreams.org/opinion/role-of-us-in-russia-ukraine-war

[9] "Like any other powerful weapon, financial sanctions should be deployed in accordance with international legal principles. That is why the G7 and the G20, together with the international financial institutions, should establish a multilateral framework to govern their use."

Subacchi, P. and Lastra, R. (2024): Financial sanctions need global governance, *Project Syndicate*. https://www.project-syndicate.org/commentary/international-framework-governing-financial-sanctions-needed-by-paola-subacchi-and-rosa-m-lastra-2024-04

[10] Russia and Ukraine held peace talks in Istanbul in March 2022. The Western literature blames Boris Johnson for scuttling a signed draft agreement. Some Russian accounts stress General Staff objections, and attribute Putin's initial receptiveness to his residual liberalism. Sachs attributes Biden's refusal to negotiate to a plot hatched by Dick Cheney to decolonize Russia in 1991.

camps portray their opponents as implacable villains and praise themselves. Both deny global hegemonic ambitions. Neither is impartial. NATO frames the armed struggle in Donbas as a war against Russian "terrorism" and expansionism; the Kremlin as self-defense against Western predation.[11] Both "boiler plate" rationalizations conceal more than they reveal.[12] They divert attention from the conflict's roots,[13] and hamper peace by fostering "dialogues of the deaf."[14]

Helmer, J. (2024): Next stage — the General Staff's targets after Putin's feint. https://johnhelmer.net/next-stage-the-general-staffs-targets-after-putins-feint/print/

Sachs, J. (2024): Why won't the US help negotiate a peaceful end to the war in Ukraine? *Common Dreams*. https://www.commondreams.org/opinion/role-of-us-in-russia-ukraine-war

[11] The International Court of Justice insists that the contest is a "civil war."

Klarenberg, K. (2024): Failed ICJ case against Russia backfires, paves way for genocide charges against Ukraine, *Mint Press*. https://www.mintpressnews.com/failed-icj-case-against-russia-backfires-paves-way-for-genocide-charges-against-ukraine/287028/

Cf. Kazdobina, J., Hedenskog, J., and Umland, A. (2024): Why the Donbas war was never "civil", *SCEEUS Report No. 6*. https://www.ui.se/globalassets/ui.se-eng/publications/other-publications/why-the-donbas-war-was-never-civil-sceeus-report-no6-2024.pdf

[12] Mate, A. (2024): How 10 years of US meddling in Ukraine undermined democracy and fueled war. https://www.aaronmate.net/p/how-10-years-of-us-meddling-in-ukraine

Hersh, S. (2024): Biden's permanent Cold War. https://seymourhersh.substack.com/p/bidens-permanent-cold-war

[13] "Then, new officials came to power in Washington who lacked historical perspective: they decided that Russia was of no account. Notably, the U.S. abrogated the 1972 Anti-Ballistic Missile Treaty — a symbol more than substance of Moscow's desire still to be seen as a great power. Then the U.S. deployed anti-ballistic missiles in Central Europe, in violation of the NATO-Russia Founding Act. For its part, Russia also took negative steps, quitting the Conventional Forces in Europe (CFE) Treaty and violating the Intermediate-Range Nuclear Forces (INF) Treaty, which led the U.S. to leave it."

"Most damaging to the chances for building shared security and avoiding a new confrontation, in 2008 President George W. Bush pressured NATO to declare that Ukraine and Georgia 'will become members of NATO.' This was clearly beyond what any major country could accept (for the U.S.: think Cuba) and violated the 1997 tacit understandings on Ukraine's position between East and West."

Hunter, R (2024): On 75th anniversary, NATO is at a serious crossroads, *Responsible State craft*. https://responsiblestatecraft.org/75th-anniversary-of-nato/.

McKern, K. (2024): Narcissus at war. https://johnmenadue.com/narcissus-at-war/

[14] The term "dialogue of the deaf" refers to a conversation or interaction in which two or more parties are unable or unwilling to truly listen or understand each other's perspectives, resulting in a lack of meaningful communication. It is often characterized by a breakdown in communication and a failure to reach a common understanding or resolution.

Washington and Moscow's hidden agendas are easily discernible. The Kremlin wants to consolidate control over Crimea, Luhansk, and Donetsk and extend its sphere of influence as far as diplomatic, economic, and military circumstances permit.[15] Putin may desire more, but is aware that expected costs are apt to be excessive.[16] Putin also wants Washington to refrain from forward deploying weapons in Ukraine that threaten Russia's homeland.[17]

Washington wants to fast-track Ukraine's NATO accession, coerce Putin's de-annexation of Crimea, restore Kyiv's control over Luhansk and

---

[15] Adrian Karatnycky contends that Putin sacrificed Viktor Yanukovych to obtain a pretext for grabbing Crimea.

Karatnycky, A. (2024): Don't buy the fringe anti-Ukraine myth about the run-up to Russia's invasion, *New York Post*. https://nypost.com/2024/05/09/opinion/dont-buy-the-fringe-anti-ukraine-myth-about-the-run-up-to-russias-invasion/

[16] Lieven, A. (2024): Nobody is competing with the U.S. to begin with, *Foreign Policy*. https://foreignpolicy.com/2024/05/01/united-states-russia-ukraine-china-taiwan-competition-primacy/.

"U.S. security elites are obsessed with the threat posed by China and Russia to U.S. global primacy. This is a serious strategic miscalculation. The United States' global network of powerful allies and bases (of which China and Russia have hardly any), unrivaled blue-water Navy, and possession of the only truly global currency mean that no other country can challenge Washington on the world stage as a whole."

Baszak, G. (2024): 'Ukraine Today Is Not a Democracy': An Interview with Former Ambassador Jack Matlock, *Antiwar*. https://original.antiwar.com/Gregor_Baszak/2024/04/30/ukraine-today-is-not-a-democracy-an-interview-with-former-ambassador-jack-matlock/

[17] "... during a Dec. 30, 2021, telephone conversation, Biden assured Putin that 'Washington had no intention of deploying offensive strike weapons in Ukraine'."

"Foreign Minister Lavrov revealed last month that when he met Antony Blinken in Geneva in January 2022, the U.S. secretary of state pretended he'd not heard of Biden's undertaking to Putin on Dec. 30, 2021. Rather, Blinken insisted that U.S. medium-range missiles could be deployed in Ukraine, and only that the U.S. might be willing to limit their number, Lavrov said."

McGovern, R. (2024): Russia & China — Two against one, *Consortium News*. https://consortiumnews.com/2024/05/17/ray-mcgovern-russia-china-two-against-one/

Donetsk, and relegate Russia to a sub-power and decolonize it.[18] President Joe Biden appreciated that Washington's end games may be risky and costly. The real battle, as he declared in his State of the Union address in March 2024, is between two Goliaths,[19] not Goliath and David. NATO

---

[18] For details, see Rosefielde, S. (2023): *Russo-Ukrainian War: Implications for the Asia Pacific*, Singapore: World Scientific, Chapter 14. For a counterview see Aron, L. (2024): What Putin's no. 2 believes about the West, *The Atlantic*. https://www.theatlantic.com/ideas/archive/2024/04/patrushev-putin-paranoia-propaganda/678220/

"The U.S. expanded its military assistance throughout 2021 (CRSR, 2022; United States Department of State, 2022), in tandem with Russian military exercises on Ukraine's eastern border, and signed the U.S.–Ukraine Charter on Strategic Partnership with Kyiv in November 2021 (Yousif, 2022), providing U.S. security commitments to Ukraine (United States Department of State, 2021). The security section of the Ukraine Charter on Strategic Partnership reads like a veiled declaration of war to restore the territorial status quo in Ukraine prior to March 2014 (United States Department of State, 2021). The combination of the Ukraine Charter on Strategic Partnership and increased lethality of expanding American military assistance to Ukraine telegraphed the United States' intention to fund and train Ukrainian forces for the recapture of Luhansk, Donetsk, and Crimea instead of relying on economic sanctions."

Lauria, J. (2024): Nato Summit: Collectively losing their minds, *Consortium News*. https://consortiumnews.com/2024/07/11/nato-summit-collectively-losing-their-minds/

The acknowledgement of NATO's aggressive intent became obvious at NATO's 75th anniversary meetings in mid-July 2024.

Aron, L. (2024): What Putin's no. 2 believes about the West, *The Atlantic*. https://www.theatlantic.com/ideas/archive/2024/04/patrushev-putin-paranoia-propaganda/678220/

[19] Biden declared in his State of the National address: "Overseas, Putin of Russia is on the march, invading Ukraine and sowing chaos throughout Europe and beyond. If anybody in this room thinks Putin will stop at Ukraine, I assure you, he will not. … We must stand up to Putin. Send me the Bipartisan National Security Bill. History is watching. If the United States walks away now, it will put Ukraine at risk. Europe at risk. The free world at risk, emboldening others who wish to do us harm. We will not walk away. We will not bow down. I will not bow down. History is watching."

Hersh, S. (2024): Biden's permanent Cold War. https://seymourhersh.substack.com/p/bidens-permanent-cold-war

and Russia fight over "redlines" to achieve their interim and long-term objectives. Washington and Moscow disagree about the interpretation of the red lines, and sometimes try to impose their own rules unilaterally.

The Kremlin grasped Biden's veiled intent from State and Defense Department documents by the fall of 2021. Putin dispatched his Foreign Minister Sergey Lavrov to persuade Biden and Antony Blinken to foreswear Ukraine's NATO accession and withdraw support for Kyiv's re-conquest of Crimea, but Washington rebuffed him, leaving Putin three options. First, he could have capitulated (rescinding Crimea's annexation). Second, he could have preempted, and third, counterattacked after a Ukrainian first strike on Luhansk, Donetsk, and Crimea. Putin chose preemption, launching a special military operation without a formal declaration of war. Biden, for diverse reasons, judged that restoring Ukraine's sovereignty over Luhansk, Donetsk, and Crimea was vital to America's national interest. Putin decided that resistance was the wisest choice. Both may ultimately rue their decisions, but neither has publicly expressed misgivings.

European NATO members were briefed that a Russo–Ukrainian proxy war was imminent, but public debate on their confidential thinking remains taboo.

Washington committed itself to act because the stakes are high. It is determined to restore Ukrainian control over Luhansk, Donetsk, and Crimea; relegate the Kremlin to a "decolonized" sub-power;[20] and preserve America's superpower monopoly. Moscow committed itself to act because it, too, considers winning vital to national security. Putin opposes relinquishing the Kremlin's sphere of influence in Ukraine, Russia's sub-power subordination and dismemberment, and desires higher international status. There is middle ground, but the White House and Putin are not yet prepared to explore it.

---

[20] Commission on Security and Cooperation in Europe, U.S. Helsinki Commission (2022): Decolonizing Russia: A moral and strategic imperative. https://www.csce.gov/briefings/decolonizing-russia-a-moral-and-strategic-imperative/

The State Department's advocacy of "decolonization" provides a moral and quasi-legal justification for promoting color revolutions in 21 non-Slavic republics of the Russian Federation.

Vohra, A. (2023): The West is preparing for Russia's disintegration. *Foreign Policy.* https://foreignpolicy.com/2023/04/17/the-west-is-preparing-for-russias-disintegration/

The impasse does not necessitate war. NATO and Russia can joust "peacefully," relying on limited gray-zone violence as they did from 2014 to 2021, while working to resolve differences. The post-Soviet Russo–American relationship started with a "partnership for peace," before souring in the new millennium. Better relations should be possible. The record reveals numerous missed opportunities for confidence building (including de-escalation) that, if seized, could have preserved the "partnership for peace" and averted the Russo–Ukrainian proxy war, and of course, both sides could have settled for peaceful coexistence.[21] Even if the East-West rivalry is endemic, war is not inexorable.

From Cold War to Partnership for Peace

The Biden administration justified the scale of its commitment to liberating Luhansk and Donetsk, reconquering Crimea, and defanging Russia by contending that the Kremlin is incorrigibly despotic, imperialist, and a dire threat to Western civilization. Washington temporizes on peace negotiations because it views compromise as appeasement.[22] The claims that Russia is an "evil empire," congenitally authoritarian, and treacherously expansionist have substance, but are overdrawn. Russia and the West are not binary civilizations. Although illiberalism, absolutism, militarism, and imperialism have been integral aspects of Russian culture for more than a millennium, liberal democratic, progressive, and socialist counter currents spawned by Europe's Renaissance, Reformation, and Enlightenment have left their mark. The Kremlin tolerates limited personal, economic, and political liberty. It understands the benefits of international cooperation. Russian leaders may desire to expand their realms, but the impulse usually is restrained by economic, political, and security counterforces.

---

[21] Kennan, G. (1960): Peaceful coexistence: A Western view, *Foreign Affairs*, Vol. 38, No. 2, 171–190.

Khrushchev, N. (1959): On peaceful coexistence, *Foreign Affairs*, Vol. 38, No 1, 1–18.

[22] "The obsession with Munich is not cost-free. Treating every dictator that the United States dislikes as if they were the reincarnation of Hitler makes it much harder to pursue intelligent compromises that might advance U.S. interests and reduce the risk of war."

Walt, S. (2024): Appeasement is underrated: Rejecting diplomacy by citing Neville Chamberlain's deal with the Nazis is a willfully ignorant use of history, *Foreign Policy*. https://foreignpolicy.com/2024/04/29/appeasement-is-underrated/

The history of transition from Soviet communism to post-socialist authoritarianism demonstrates that the Kremlin is neither inextricably wedded to despotism nor imperial expansion. Russia partially democratized, liberalized, de-imperialized, and integrated into the American-led world order as Washington counseled during the late 1980s and 1990s, before broken promises, mutual suspicions, and jousting over spheres of influence derailed the Russo–American partnership for peace.[23]

Mikhail Gorbachev led the charge against despotism and the Soviet empire. He fostered radical economic reform (*perestroika*), democratization (*demokratizatsiya*), "new thinking" (*novoe politicheskoe myshlenie*), openness (*otkritnost*), and disarmament.[24] He permitted Soviet republics to secede, relinquished control over the Warsaw Pact and CMEA (Council for Mutual Economic Assistance), and slashed weapons procurement by 90%.

His successors accepted Washington's "Grand Bargain."[25] They continued Gorbachev's market transition,[26] arms restraint, and passively assented to former Warsaw Pact members joining the European Union and

---

[23] Russia joined the Partnership for Peace program on May 27, 1997.

Eckel, M. (2021): Did the West promise Moscow that NATO would not expand? Well, it's complicated. *Radio Free Europe*. https://www.rferl.org/a/nato-expansion-russia-mislead/31263602.html

[24] Gorbachev, M. (1987): *Perestroika: New Thinking for Our Country and the World*, New York: Harper & Row.

[25] George Bush and Bill Clinton promised Boris Yeltsin a "Grand Bargain, lavish Western financial and technical assistance in return for Russia's commitment to embrace democracy, freehold private property, competitive markets, free trade, direct foreign investment, disarmament, and G-7 tutelage regarding EU and NATO expansion."

Rosefielde. S. (1994): *Benign Neglect: The Benefits and Risks of Japan's Minimalist Russian Assistance Program*, Kyoto: Annual Bulletin of The Research Institute for Social Science, Ryukoku University.

Rosefielde, S. (1994). Peace and Prosperity in the Pacific Rim: Optimizing the Benefits of Japanese Assistance to Russia, *Acta Slavica Iaponica*, Vol. 12, 47–61.

Allison, G. and Blackwill. R. (1991). America's Stake in the Soviet Future, *Foreign Affairs*, Vol. 70, No. 3: 77–97.

[26] Yeltsin called the program *"perekhod,"* which means "transition" from Soviet authoritarian planning to Western liberal democratic free enterprise.

NATO but back-tracked on democracy during the 1993 constitutional crisis over "shock therapy."[27]

Neither Boris Yeltsin nor Putin sought to rebuild and modernize Russia's armed forces before 2001.[28] Both opposed the resurrection of the Soviet Union, communist power, Marxism-Leninism, and central economic planning. They supported privatization and workably competitive markets, and refrained from voicing irredentist claims against Ukraine.

Taking these diverse accomplishments into account, Andrei Shleifer and Daniel Treisman famously declared in 2005 that Russia had become a "normal" middle-income developing country.[29] Although many experts harbored doubts,[30] no NATO spokesperson voiced concern that Russia might soon degenerate into an expansionist, authoritarian, martial police state with a dysfunctional anti-competitive economy.

---

[27] The Speaker of the Russian Supreme Soviet, Ruslan Khasbulatov, opposed shock therapy reforms. He was an obstacle to the Gaidar-Group of 7 (G7) transition program. Yeltsin reacted by disbanding the Supreme Soviet and Congress of People's Deputies on September 21, 1993, and ruling by decree until the election of the new parliament and a referendum on a new constitution, triggering a constitutional crisis. The Supreme Soviet counter attacked by removing Yeltsin from the presidency for breaching the constitution, and Yeltsin retaliated by having the army shell the Russian White House (parliament building). The shelling killed 187 people.

Candidates supporting Yeltsin's economic policies were resoundingly defeated in the ensuing December 1993 elections. However, the referendum approved a new constitution, significantly expanding Yeltsin's powers to appoint government officials, dismiss the prime minister, and dissolve the Duma. Yeltsin ruled autocratically thereafter, paying scant attention to parliament. There were subsequent elections, but many considered them rigged. The G7, World Bank, and International Monetary Fund (IMF) celebrated Russian elections as a great victory for Western parliamentary democracy, until Putin annexed Crimea. Today, Washington condemns Russian elections as shams, and Putin as a despot. Post-Soviet Russian authoritarian democracy is a step forward from pre-Gorbachev Soviet regimes, but is still a major disappointment.

Bill Clinton's support for Yeltsin's strong presidency facilitated Russia's authoritarian revival.

[28] Rosefielde, S. (2023): *Russo–Ukrainian War: Implications for the Asia Pacific*, Singapore: World Scientific, Chapter 5.

[29] Shleifer, A. and Treisman, D. (2005): A Normal Country: Russia After Communism, *Journal of Economic Perspectives*, Vol. 19, No. 1, 151–174. https://pubs.aeaweb.org/doi/pdfplus/10.1257/0895330053147949

[30] Rosefielde, S. (2005): Russia: An Abnormal Country, *European Journal of Comparative Economics*, Vol. 2, No. 1, 3–16.

Even though Gorbachev, Yeltsin, and Putin complained about NATO expansion, and Russia suffered grievously from World Bank-endorsed economic "shock therapy" from 1987 to 2000,[31] the Kremlin in 2005

---

[31] Rosefielde, S. (2023): *Russo-Ukrainian War: Implications for the Asia Pacific*, Singapore: World Scientific, Chapter 3.

Sachs, J. (2000): Russia's tumultuous decade: An insider remembers, *The Washington Monthly*. https://web.archive.org/web/20000407085843/http://www.washingtonmonthly.com/books/2000/0003.sachs.html

"Shock" entailed sudden and complete termination of government support for all economic activities. Necessity was said to be the mother of invention. Faced with destitution, shock therapists like Jeffrey Sachs contended that former state managers and workers would find a path to wealth-generating entrepreneurial competition. Yeltsin heeded Washington's advice, choosing to rely on World Bank, IMF, and G7 advice, haphazardly implemented by his cronies, (kleptocrats, oligarchs), officials, secret police, military commanders, and the mafia avidly began rent-seeking and privatizing state assets to themselves. The ensuing mayhem plunged Russia into hyperinflation and hyper-depression (deeper than the 1929 American Great Depression). Barter replaced money exchange (virtual economy). The reforms devastated living standards of much of the population, especially groups dependent on Soviet-era state subsidies and welfare programs, but Yeltsin did not despair. He stayed his course until the day he left office, believing that tomorrow would be a brighter day, while most Russians acutely suffered. A quarter of the population was unemployed, and 3.4 million died prematurely. Income and wealth inequality skyrocketed.

Rosefielde, S. (2023): *Russo-Ukrainian War: Implications for the Asia Pacific*. Singapore: World Scientific.

Goldman, M. (1992): *The Piratization of Russia: Russian Reform Goes Awry*, London: Routledge.

In late 1992, Yeltsin launched a program of free vouchers as a way to give mass privatization a jump start. Under the program, all Russian citizens were issued vouchers, each with a nominal value of around 10,000 rubles, for the purchase of shares of select state enterprises. Although each citizen initially received a voucher of equal face value, within months the majority of them converged in the hands of intermediaries who were ready to buy them for cash right away. In 1995, Yeltsin prepared for a new wave of privatization, offering stock shares in some of Russia's most valuable state enterprises in exchange for bank loans. The program was promoted as a way of simultaneously speeding up privatization and ensuring the government a cash infusion to cover its operating needs. It was a swindle. The deals gave away valuable state assets to a small group of tycoons in finance, industry, energy, telecommunications, and the media who came to be known as "oligarchs" in the mid-1990s. By mid-1996, substantial ownership shares over major firms were acquired at very low prices by a handful of people. Boris Berezovsky, who controlled major stakes in several banks and the national media, emerged as one of Yeltsin's most prominent supporters. Along with Berezovsky were Mikhail Khodorkovsky, Vladimir Potanin, Vladimir Bogdanov, Rem Viakhirev, Vagit Alekperov, Alexander Smolensky, Viktor Vekselberg, and Mikhail Fridman, and a few years later Roman Abramovich.

appeared to be a worthy post-Soviet, Group of Eight "partner for peace" despite serious latent grievances.[32]

Galeoti, M. (2018): *The Vory Russia's Super Mafia*, New Haven: Yale University Press.

The vory, as the Russian mafia is also known, was born early in the 20th century, largely in the gulags and criminal camps, where they developed their unique culture. Identified by their signature tattoos, members abided by the thieves' code, a strict system that forbade all paid employment and cooperation with law enforcement and the state.

Russia's hyper-depression hit all economic sectors. The American Great Depression was concentrated in investment. Aggregate consumption was unchanged.

Rosefielde, S., Danilin, V., and Kleiner, G. (1994): "Deistvuiushaya Model' Reform i Ugroza Giperdepressii" (The Russian Reform Model and the Threat of Hyperdepression), *Russian Economic Journal* (*Rossiiskii Ekonomicheskii Zhurnal*), No. 12, 48–55.

Nixon, R. (1994): Letter to President William Clinton. (Secret. Declassified.)

Sachs, J. (2000): Russia's tumultuous decade: An insider remembers, The *Washington Monthly*. https://web.archive.org/web/20000407085843/http://www.washingtonmonthly.com/books/2000/0003.sachs.html

Dawisha, K. (2014): *Putin's Kleptocracy: Who Owns Russia?* New York: Simon & Schuster.

Gaddy C. and Ickes, B. (2002): *Russia's Virtual Economy*, Washington D.C.: Brookings Institution Press.

Ericson R. and Ickes, B. (2003): A model of Russia's "virtual economy," in: Ichiishi, T., Marschak, T. (eds.), *Markets, Games, and Organizations: Essays in Honor of Roy Radner*, Berlin: Springer.

Gerber T. and Hout, M. (1998): More Shock than Therapy: Market Transition, Employment, and Income in Russia, 1991–1995, *American Journal of Sociology*, Vol. 104, No. 1, 1–50.

Field M. and Twigg, J. (eds.) (2000): *Russia's Torn Safety Nets*, New York: St. Martin's Press.

In February 1992, Russia's vice president Alexander Rutskoy denounced the Yeltsin program as "economic genocide."

Bohlen, C. (1992): Yeltsin deputy calls reforms 'economic genocide,' *The New York Times*. https://www.nytimes.com/1992/02/09/world/yeltsin-deputy-calls-reforms-economic-genocide.html

Rosefielde, S. (2000): The Civilian Labor Force and Unemployment in the Russian Federation, *Europe-Asia Studies*, Vol. 52, No. 8, 1433–1447.

Rosefielde, S. (2001): Premature Deaths: Russia's Radical Transition, *Europe-Asia Studies*, Vol. 53, No. 8, 1159–1176.

Ghodsee, K. (2017): *Red Hangover: Legacies of Twentieth-Century Communism*, North Carolina: Duke University Press.

Scheidel, W. (2017): *The Great Leveler: Violence and the History of Inequality from the Stone Age to the Twenty-First Century*, New Jersey: Princeton University Press.

[32] Rosefielde, S. (2023): *Russo-Ukrainian War: Implications for the Asia Pacific*. Singapore: World Scientific.

From Partnership for Peace to Proxy War

Russia's unexpected economic recovery from 1998 to 2007,[33] the military modernization program (which began in 2001),[34] the 2008 global financial crisis,[35] and Foggy Bottom's decision to press Ukraine's accession to NATO in 2008 combined to adjust Moscow and Washington's attitudes toward their partnership for peace.[36] Russia's economic recovery ignited Kremlin hopes that Russia could restore its superpower, a prospect that may have encouraged George Bush to accelerate Ukraine's NATO accession. The global financial crisis, its lingering adverse aftermath, and Russia's surprisingly successful weapons modernization drive increased Western anxieties.[37] These events bolstered Putin's confidence that Russia could restore its lost superpower and aroused mutual suspicions, nudging Moscow and Washington sequentially from partnership toward Cold Peace (2008–2014), Cold War (2014–2022), and Proxy War (2022–2024). The turning points were George Bush's advocacy of Ukraine's NATO accession at the NATO 2008 Bucharest Summit,[38] the Euromaidan 2014 color revolution, the Russiagate imbroglio,[39] and Russia's 2022 special military operation (invasion of Ukraine).

---

[33] Rosefielde, S. (2023): *Russo-Ukrainian War: Implications for the Asia Pacific*. Singapore: World Scientific, Chapter 4.

[34] Rosefielde, S. (2023): *Russo-Ukrainian War: Implications for the Asia Pacific*. Singapore: World Scientific, Chapter 5.

[35] Rosefielde, S., Kuboniwa, M., and Mizobata, S. (2012): *Prevention and Crisis Management: Lessons for Asia from the 2008 Crisis*, Singapore: World Scientific.

[36] Rosefielde, S. (2023): *Russo-Ukrainian War: Implications for the Asia Pacific*. Singapore: World Scientific.

[37] Western media ignored Russia's arms modernization initiative, but Russia published details readily available to Western think tanks, defense analysis, the United States Defense Intelligence Agency, and the Central Intelligence Agency responsible for monitoring Russian military activities.

[38] Harding, L. (2008): Bush backs Ukraine and Georgia for NATO membership, *The Guardian*. https://www.theguardian.com/world/2008/apr/01/nato.georgia

[39] The American Democratic Party, infuriated by what it considered the Russian government's attempt to sabotage Hillary Clinton presidential prospects for Donald Trump's benefit, became publicly hostile toward the Kremlin.

Boyd-Barrett, O. and Marmura, S. (2023): *Russiagate Revisited: The Aftermath of a Hoax*, New York: Palgrave Macmillan.

Confrontation

Washington's fateful decision to restore Ukraine's territorial integrity and accelerate Kyiv's NATO accession in November 2021 set America firmly on the proxy war path but did not fix the strike date. Biden had the ability to manage the confrontation by offering the Kremlin concessions on Ukraine's NATO accession, slowing arms shipments to Kyiv, and relaxing economic sanctions. He chose not to make any of these concessions, instead sounding the alarm that Putin was on the cusp of invading Ukraine in early February 2022. Apparently, Biden was confident that, when confronted with strong Western resolve, the Kremlin would withdraw from Luhansk and Donetsk, de-annex Crimea, and grudgingly accept Ukraine's NATO accession, or if Moscow chose to fight it would be swiftly defeated. He misjudged on both scores, and Washington has yet to adjust by offering concessions on Ukraine's NATO accession, tapering arms shipments to Kyiv, and softening economic sanctions.[40] Instead, the West has upped the stakes by transforming NATO from a defensive into an offensive institution in July 2024.[41] NATO could be escalating to de-escalate, but even if this is the intention, bureaucratic inertia will impede NATO's reversion to its traditional defensive posture.

Rapprochement and Settlement

If Ukrainian armed forces defeat Russia on the battlefield or the Kremlin capitulates for other reasons, Washington will achieve its objectives in Ukraine. If the Russo–Ukrainian proxy war morphs into prolonged East–West hot war, then America and Europe must expand their military industrial capabilities and reduce social programs, but may be unable to do either, incurring potentially dire consequences.

If the conflict is frozen, or Ukraine collapses, NATO will be compelled to mitigate damage by bilaterally (US–Russia) negotiating spheres of influence and economic sanctions disputes, and trilaterally

---

[40] Aron, L. (2024): What Putin's no. 2 believes about the West, *The Atlantic*. https://www.theatlantic.com/ideas/archive/2024/04/patrushev-putin-paranoia-propaganda/678220/

[41] Beebe, G. (2024): We need a rational discussion about the Russian threat, *Responsible Statecraft*. https://responsiblestatecraft.org/russia-threat/

Lauria, J. (2024): Nato Summit: Collectively losing their minds, *Consortium News*. https://consortiumnews.com/2024/07/11/nato-summit-collectively-losing-their-minds/

(US–Ukraine–Russia) settling territorial and reparation claims, vouchsafed with security guarantees.[42]

Attitude adjustment is the foundation stone for peacefully resolving NATO–Russian sphere of influence disputes. Washington and Moscow must replace the conviction that they are implacable enemies with the premise that they can peacefully coexist, mutually accommodating one another on the rules of Cold War engagement including alliances, color revolutions, forward military deployments, tactical nuclear employment, weapons of mass destruction, economic sanctions, frozen assets, impoundment, reparations, gray-zone intrigue, frozen conflicts, and annexation. Once Washington and Moscow reach a meeting of the minds on these fundamentals, NATO, Ukraine, and Russia can trilaterally negotiate a final Russo-Ukrainian War settlement.

Third Parties

Russia, NATO, and Ukraine are combatants. Their actions govern the Russo–Ukrainian War and final settlement, but outcomes partly depend on the behavior of other nations. Third parties may supply arms and components, comply with economic sanctions, affect public attitudes, and realign global power, diversely affecting battlefield results and settlement strategies.

The world is polarized on these issues. Western non-NATO countries provide Ukraine with material support. They comply with American and EU economic sanctions and endorse Biden's characterization of the Russo–Ukrainian War. The "Global South" avoids condemning Russia,[43] expresses some appreciation for Putin's concerns, and often evades compliance with Western economic sanctions, despite Washington's imposition of secondary sanctions.[44] North Korea and Iran provide the Kremlin

---

[42] The proxy war between NATO and Russia is about spheres of influence and the implicit rules of Cold War engagement. Principals must resolve power sharing disputes between themselves, a task most addressable prior to trilateral final proxy war settlement.

[43] According to the United Nations Conference on Trade and Development, the Global South broadly comprises Africa, Latin America and the Caribbean, Asia (excluding Israel, Japan, and South Korea), and Oceania (excluding Australia and New Zealand).

[44] U.S. Department of the Treasury (2024): As Russia completes transition to a full war economy, Treasury takes sweeping aim at foundational financial infrastructure and access to third country support. https://home.treasury.gov/news/press-releases/jy2404

with weapons. Beijing exports technology and components to Moscow. Others including China help Russia circumvent SWIFT (Society for Worldwide Interbank Financial Telecommunications) international payment restrictions.

The strength of a victory for either side will scale power benefits for principals directly, supporters derivatively, and may allow some nations like Iran, Turkey, and India improved possibilities for plying independent paths. The terms of final settlement may significantly affect the correlation of global forces.[45]

Merit

There is a wide array of plausible Russo–Ukrainian War outcomes for principals and third parties. Their merit lies diversely in the eyes of beholders. Principals and third parties will strive to optimize under constraint, while sundry stakeholders judge merit according to their druthers. Each will try to persuade skeptics that their view is right, with varying success. There is apt to be a short list of influential postmortems, but only limited consensus on a handful of facts and predictions. Ukraine will or will not restore its sovereignty over its pre-Maiden territory. Russia will or will not retain control over Crimea. History will judge whether sledgehammer economic sanctions were decisive and Biden's confrontation strategy fulfilled his predictions.

Prospects

The Democratic Party establishment and Trump populists hold diametrically opposed attitudes toward the Russo–Ukrainian proxy war. Democrats and the non-populist faction of the Republican Party take a victory or death approach to the proxy war. They say that NATO will fight and win a nuclear war if push comes to shove. Trump, without debating the rights and wrongs of the conflict, insists that if he had been president at the start of 2022, he would have cut an amicable deal with Putin averting the war.

---

[45] Correlation of forces is a Soviet concept, with general applicability that weighs the comparative military, economic, political, social, and ideological factors determining the balance of international power.

Trump is certainly right. If he had been president in 2021, he would have curtailed American military assistance to Ukraine and precluded Kyiv's accession to NATO. Putin would not have launched his special military operation, and the proxy war never would have started. Trump warned in July 2024 that if Harris wins the presidential election, there is apt to be a "Third World War."[46] The risk is real.

The Biden administration, and now Harris, by contrast, are determined to keep fighting until the war ends on better terms than Putin now is willing to offer.[47] Putin recently elaborated his settlement terms. They were too rich for the Biden–Harris team who claims that they will fight the war forever if necessary or until victory is theirs. By contrast, substantial concessions are not essential for Trump to cut a deal.[48] He is likely to do just that, if elected. The NATO establishment considers such a deal unwise. There is a chance that it is right, but there is no room for doubt that Trump can and probably will negotiate a peace settlement, if elected.

Although voters may judge otherwise, prospects for peace under a Harris presidency are dim. The tea leaves point to a prolonged Russo–Ukrainian War of attrition,[49] ending not with a bang, but a

---

[46] Anders, C. (2024): Trump warns Netanyahu of 'third world war' if he loses US election, *Semafor*. https://www.semafor.com/article/07/26/2024/trump-warns-netanyahu-of-third-world-war-if-he-loses-us-election

[47] McFaul, M. (2024): Vice President Harris's views on the war in Ukraine, Russia, and Belarus. https://michaelmcfaul.substack.com/p/vice-president-harriss-views-on-the

[48] Vazquez, M. and DeYoung, K. (2024): Vance says Trump's plan to end war in Ukraine could include creating demilitarized zone, *Washington Post*. https://www.washingtonpost.com/politics/2024/09/12/vance-trump-ukraine-russia-war-plan/

[49] Johnson, L. (2024): Western generals and pundits still traffic in false assumptions about Russia. https://larryjohnson.substack.com/p/western-generals-and-pundits-still

Johnson cites Colonel Alex Vershinin.

Vershinin, A. (2024): The attritional art of war: Lessons from the Russian war on Ukraine. *RUSI*. https://www.rusi.org/explore-our-research/publications/commentary/attritional-art-war-lessons-russian-war-ukraine

"Attritional wars require their own 'Art of War' and are fought with a 'force-centric' approach, unlike wars of manoeuvre which are 'terrain-focused'. They are rooted in massive industrial capacity to enable the replacement of losses, geographical depth to absorb a series of defeats, and technological conditions that prevent rapid ground movement. In attritional wars, military operations are shaped by a state's ability to replace losses and generate new formations, not tactical and operational manoeuvres. The side that accepts the attritional nature of war and focuses on destroying enemy forces rather than gaining terrain is most likely to win.

whimper,[50] protestations to the contrary notwithstanding.[51] It is wishful thinking to expect providence to pull NATO's chestnuts out of the fire.[52] Exiting the quagmire on terms the Biden administration considers palatable will not be easy.[53]

"The West is not prepared for this kind of war. To most Western experts, attritional strategy is counterintuitive. Historically, the West preferred the short 'winner takes all' clash of professional armies. Recent war games such as CSIS's war over Taiwan covered one month of fighting. The possibility that the war would go on never entered the discussion. This is a reflection of a common Western attitude. Wars of attrition are treated as exceptions, something to be avoided at all costs and generally products of leaders' ineptitude. Unfortunately, wars between near-peer powers are likely to be attritional, thanks to a large pool of resources available to replace initial losses. The attritional nature of combat, including the erosion of professionalism due to casualties, levels the battlefield no matter which army started with better trained forces. As conflict drags on, the war is won by economies, not armies. States that grasp this and fight such a war via an attritional strategy aimed at exhausting enemy resources while preserving their own are more likely to win. The fastest way to lose a war of attrition is to focus on manoeuvre, expending valuable resources on near-term territorial objectives. Recognising that wars of attrition have their own art is vital to winning them without sustaining crippling losses."

[50] T. S. Eliot, "The Hollow Man." https://allpoetry.com/the-hollow-men

"This is the way the world ends
This is the way the world ends
This is the way the world ends
Not with a bang but a whimper."

[51] "Washington and Kiev are negotiating a bilateral security agreement that mirrors the 10-year commitments Ukraine has entered into with several European powers."

Devlin, B. (2024): The Biden Admin is trying to guarantee a forever war in Ukraine, *The American Conservative*. https://www.theamericanconservative.com/the-biden-admin-is-trying-to-guarantee-a-forever-war-in-ukraine/

[52] Rutland, P. (2024): A Putin collapse? The dangers of wishful thinking, *Responsible Statecraft*. https://responsiblestatecraft.org/putin-russia-collapse/

Cockburn, A. (2024): How our military has helped push Ukraine toward defeat. https://spoilsofwar.substack.com/p/how-our-military-has-helped-push

[53] The *siloviki* (power services) are unlikely to forget that the transition strategy foisted on Gorbachev and Yeltsin was catastrophic and may have been pressed with malicious intent. Also see Lozansky, E. (2024): Recollections of an event participant: A game with great hopes, *Pluralia*. https://pluralia.forumverona.com/en/a/recollections-of-an-event-participant-a-game-with-great-hopes/

"Even when Russia was ready to play such a role under President Boris Yeltsin, whom Bill Clinton called his best friend and helped win elections in 1996, it was Clinton who betrayed him by starting an anti-Russia crusade in 1998 through NATO Eastern expansion despite Western pledge to previous President Michail Gorbachev not to move NATO 'one inch East.' When Vladimir Putin entered the Kremlin and dared to demand that Russia's interests also should be taken into account Washington was not very happy, but there were some glimpses of hope at the end of 2001 when President George W. Bush praised Putin for his help in the Afghan operation after 9/11. Bush not only warmly welcomed him in Washington but also in his home state, Texas, where he called Putin 'a great Russian leader' in front of Crawford High School students, with whom America is ready to build a brighter future.

"Putin believed him, and in turn, during the follow-up Russian Embassy reception, said that Russia is prepared for U.S.-Russia rapprochement as close as the U.S. is ready. After the official part, Republican Congressman Curt Weldon and I walked to Putin and presented him with the working plan for such a rapprochement, titled 'U.S.-Russia Partnership: A New Time, A New Beginning'.

"This plan included cooperation in space, the environment, agriculture, energy, public health and medicine, infectious diseases, earth sciences, information technology, education culture and a wide range of basic science disciplines.

"It included the list of government and private organizations plus individuals responsible for implementation of these proposals and the letter to President Bush signed by over 100 Members of Congress who endorsed this document…

"Regrettably, it didn't take long for GW to betray Putin by starting a 'democracy promotion' crusade through color revolutions in post-Soviet space, supporting Ukraine's Orange revolution, abrogating the Anti-Ballistic-Missile (ABM) treaty, and most devastating push for Georgia and Ukraine into NATO.

"Obama started his term with a highly advertised 'reset,' meaning opening a comprehensive dialogue with Russia, which aligned with our above-mentioned proposal. Unfortunately, this initiative also very quickly collapsed both symbolically and in reality. When U.S. Secretary of State Hillary Clinton presented Russian Foreign Minister Sergei Lavrov with a red 'reset' button to symbolize the intention to improve ties, the word 'reset' was mistranslated into Russian for 'overcharge.' What was it? An offer of cooperation or a red alert?

"In reality, things went from bad to worse after Obama gave the Ukrainian portfolio to his Vice-President Joe Biden, who, according to former Defense Secretary Bob Gates, over the past four decades, had been 'wrong on nearly every major foreign policy and national security issue.'

"We don't know if Obama was sincere in his attempt to improve U.S.-Russia relations, but wittingly or unwittingly, he also betrayed the cause for peace by placing Biden in charge of U.S. policy on Ukraine since according to many observers, he is the one who is responsible for the current crisis.

"First, he coordinated the February 2014 coup in Ukraine that brought a pro-NATO regime in Kyiv, then robbed this unfortunate country to make money via his son Hunter, then rejected Russia's December 2021 proposal to start mutual security guarantees' negotiations, then together with British Prime Minister Boris Johnson disrupted ready for signing Russia-Ukraine agreement to end the war. Instead, now Biden is using his presidential powers to prolong it with more U.S. taxpayer money."

Chapter 13

NATO

The North Atlantic Treaty Organization (NATO) is an intergovernmental military alliance of 32 member states — 30 European and two North American. Established in the aftermath of World War II, the organization implements the North Atlantic Treaty, signed in Washington, D.C., on April 4, 1949. NATO is a collective security system; its independent member states agree to defend each other against attacks by third parties. During the Cold War, NATO operated as a check on the threat posed by the Soviet Union.

There is little opposition to the organization, and it is apt to play only a small role in swaying voters in the 2024 presidential election, but this could change if Trump fully exploits the possibilities. Opposition to NATO in the 20th century came mostly from pacifist organizations, workers movements, environmental groups, and socialist and communist political parties. Many of them contended that NATO endangered global peace and stability, was environmentally destructive, and an obstacle to nuclear disarmament. There was also some periodic discussion of whether the European Union should develop its own military capability.[1]

Some suggested that NATO should have been disbanded after the Soviet Union dissolved because it no longer served a useful purpose, until its members conjured up new missions. NATO supporters rose to the challenge by reconceiving the institution as a "cooperative security"

---

[1] Franke, U. (2024): The never-ending debate of the European Army and why it is unhelpful, *Heinrich Böll Stiftung*. https://www.boell.de/en/2024/01/22/never-ending-debate-european-army-and-why-it-unhelpful

organization with a dual mandate: fostering dialogue with former Warsaw Pact adversaries and managing conflicts in areas on the European periphery, such as the Balkans. In keeping with the first objective, NATO established the North Atlantic Cooperation Council to provide a forum for the exchange of views on political and security issues, as well as the Partnership for Peace (PfP) program in 1994 to enhance European security and stability through joint military training exercises with NATO and non-NATO states, including the former Soviet republics. Special links were also set up with Russia and Ukraine. NATO was considered innocuous until the Balkan War in 1999.

The organization was never politically divisive during and after the Soviet era, although some doubted whether its benefits justified the cost to American taxpayers. The issue first came to the public's attention in 2016 when Donald Trump accused European and Canadian NATO members of freeloading. He threatened to withdraw from NATO if elected president unless Europeans paid their fair share of expenses. He did not act on his promise but remains skeptical of NATO's geostrategic worth.

The Democratic Party never echoed Trump's misgivings and has remained a stalwart NATO supporter for 75 years.

Nonetheless, the issue could take on greater importance in the November 2024 election because NATO today has morphed into an entirely new alliance. Until July 2024, NATO proclaimed that it was solely a defensive alliance. Now it embraces an offensive mission, not just against Russia, but against adversaries across the globe including China.[2]

Trump could seize the day. He has repeatedly said that as soon as he becomes president again, he will negotiate an end to the Russo–Ukrainian War. If he continues to repeat the pledge, he may justify it by pointing out that not only are many Europeans NATO free riders, but NATO is becoming a menace to world peace, forcing Harris to explain why she believes

---

[2]Leonard, M. (2024): A new EU shaped by war, *Foreign Policy*. https://foreignpolicy.com/2024/07/01/europe-us-nato-russia-war-geopolitics/

Sikorski, R. (2024): Deterring Russia is cheaper than war, *Foreign Policy*. https://foreignpolicy.com/2024/07/01/europe-eu-russia-war-deterrence-military-nato-spending-geopolitics-blocs/

it is wise to contemplate spending trillions of dollars to defeat the East militarily without giving diplomacy a fair chance. It will be difficult to persuade voters that the financial costs and risks of global thermonuclear war are worth shunning diplomacy. The Bulletin of the Atomic Scientists estimates that a modest nuclear exchange will kill 5.4 billion people.[3]

If NATO continues morphing in an offensive direction, is it reasonable to suppose that the West will win a prolonged Russo–Ukrainian War when it refuses to modify its military industrial strategy and match Moscow's arsenal? The answer is probably no, because precedent suggests that NATO is likely to fail to design, build, and pay for forces needed to counter Russia's replenished armed forces in Ukraine, to say nothing about deterring China. If Russia deploys larger armies on the Ukrainian battlefield, and its military industrial complex agilely designs, innovates, and replaces equipment losses, NATO strategic patience will not carry the day. Russia and China will outgun and outman NATO, because the West's deterrence philosophy and peacetime politics preclude efficient weapons acquisition and the maintenance of a large standing army.[4] Ceteris paribus, if NATO tries to compete with Russia and China, it will only be able to procure small batches of high-unit-cost weapons and small armies

---

[3] Bulletin of the Atomic Scientists. (2024): Nowhere to hide: How a nuclear war would kill you — and almost everyone else. https://thebulletin.org/2022/10/nowhere-to-hide-how-a-nuclear-war-would-kill-you-and-almost-everyone-else/

National Security Archive (2022): Long-classified U.S. estimates of nuclear war casualties during the Cold War regularly underestimated deaths and destruction. https://nsarchive.gwu.edu/briefing-book/nuclear-vault/2022-07-14/long-classified-us-estimates-nuclear-war-casualties-during

Tegmark, M. (2023): Here's how bad a nuclear war would actually be, *Time*. https://time.com/6290977/nuclear-war-impact-essay/

[4] Politics distorts threat assessments and all aspects of efficiently meeting military challenges. The result is an excessively high-cost, inflexible establishment that has difficulty coping with a wide array of threats.

insufficient to defeat the East,[5] and too expensive to justify the domestic political cost.[6]

Vladimir Putin and Xi Jinping fully grasp that the West is stronger on paper, but also know from experience that Washington and Brussels delude themselves believing that half-trying is good enough. Political complacency and foot dragging could be NATO's undoing.[7]

Kamala Harris does not get it. Trump intuits the danger.[8]

---

[5] Office of the Director of National Intelligence (2024): Annual threat assessment of the U.S. Intelligence community. https://www.dni.gov/files/ODNI/documents/assessments/ATA-2024-Unclassified-Report.pdf

Atlamazoglou, S. (2024): The US intelligence community assesses the state of the Russian military, *Sandboxx*. https://www.sandboxx.us/news/the-us-intelligence-community-assesses-the-state-of-the-russian-military/

"The Russian military has managed to somewhat flip the tables in Ukraine. Acute shortages in ammunition — particularly artillery rounds — have made the Ukrainian forces much weaker. As a result, the Russian forces have been gaining ground in eastern Ukraine and the Donbas. The trajectory of the conflict shows that the Russian military can withstand some serious punishment for long periods. Russia's political system facilitates this capacity to endure losses and operational setbacks. Thus, in a potential war with Russia, the U.S. and NATO would have to account for an adversary that could bounce back from what would otherwise have been catastrophic failures and miscalculations."

[6] Cohen, P. and Alderman, L. (2024): Europe wants to build a stronger defense industry, but can't decide how, *The New York Times*. https://www.nytimes.com/2024/05/20/business/economy/europe-defense-spending.html

Sachs, J. (2024): The NATO declaration and the deadly strategy of neoconservatism, *Common Dreams*. https://www.commondreams.org/opinion/nato-neoconservatism-empire

[7] Sachs, M. (2024): The NATO declaration and the deadly strategy of neoconservatism, *Common Dreams*. https://www.commondreams.org/opinion/nato-neoconservatism-empire

[8] Sachs, M. (2024): The NATO declaration and the deadly strategy of neoconservatism, *Common Dreams*. https://www.commondreams.org/opinion/nato-neoconservatism-empire

Chapter 14

China

During much of the post-World War II era, elite Democratic Party progressives sympathized with Mao Zedong's revolutionary communism and lamented the humiliations inflicted on 19th-century China. They, together with sections of America's business community, supported China's admission to the World Trade Organization (WTO) in 2001 and persuaded themselves that China was destined to be progressive America's partner for peace and prosperity. Both saw no commercial or military storm clouds on the horizon, and confidently predicted that China would democratize and rapidly develop. Experience proved them prescient about modernization and purblind on democracy, unfettered free trade, and militarization.[1]

The World Bank today classifies China as an upper middle-income country.[2] Beijing, Shanghai, Guangzhou, Xiamen, and Chengdu are modern megalopolises, far more livable than their American counterparts. But China remains a one-party authoritarian communist state, foreign trade manipulator, and formidable military rival committed to annexing Taiwan, transgressing its neighbors' seabed mineral rights, unilaterally settling disputed territorial claims in the South China Sea, dominating the Straits of Malacca, expanding its global reach through the Belt and Road Initiative, and oppressing the Uighurs and Tibetans. It is in the process of

---

[1] Rosefielde, S. (2023): *Socialist Economic Systems: 21st Century Pathways*, London: Routledge, Chapter 16.
[2] World Bank Group: The World Bank in China: Overview. https://www.worldbank.org/en/country/china/overview

forging a powerful military and commercial coalition with Russia and is a staunch source of support for communist North Korea.

China's rapidly growing military threat to Western interests is grasped and accepted in Washington and the North Atlantic Treaty Organization, but the American Defense Department, hobbled by Congress, is doing little about it.[3] Real defense spending has been declining for a decade, and America is on the cusp of losing its military technology edge.

The same story holds for China's unfair trading, although it is unclear whether Kamala Harris or Donald Trump fully comprehend the challenge. The Biden administration and Trump seem to believe that because China today is a market economy, they can gauge the magnitude of Beijing's unfair trading from public data on tariffs and quotas, and monitoring China trade surplus. These indicators are important; however, they do not capture the distortions concealed by China's state economic management system. Enterprises classified as private by Chinese authorities are not actually private. There is no private freehold property over tangible productive assets. The entire means of Chinese production is the freehold property of the people managed by the Communist Party and its state apparatus. This is why China remains a Marxist-Leninist communist economic system.

Xi Jinping's regime classifies property as state, provincial, municipal, and private based on the majority owner of leasehold shares. For example, if private entities own the majority leasehold shares, the government classifies the leasehold as private, even though the underlying freehold rights belong entirely to the state which dictates the terms of leasehold contracts, including managerial compensation. The only reward private investors get from financing their leasehold business is the control and compensation rights the Communist Party chooses to give them. The principle applies for state (where the state owns more than 50% of the leasehold), provincial, and municipal leaseholds. The State-owned Assets Supervision

---

[3] Rand Corporation is pushing low cost anti-ship drones as a cost efficient solution to Beijing's challenge. It is premature to assess this development.

  Kallenborn, Z. and Plichta, M. (2024): Breaking the shield: Countering drone defenses, *National Defense University Press.* https://digitalcommons.ndu.edu/cgi/viewcontent.cgi?article=1004&context=joint-force-quarterly

  Doyle, G. and Stone, M. (2024): US strategy for anti-ship weapons to counter China: plentiful, mobile, deadly, *Reuters.* https://www.reuters.com/business/aerospace-defense/us-strategy-anti-ship-weapons-counter-china-plentiful-mobile-deadly-2024-09-17/

and Administration Commission of the State Council supervises leaseholds of all types.[4]

Lease contracts, Communist Party supervisors, government contracts, mandates, and regulations govern the behavior of Chinese enterprise managers, allowing the Communist Party to invisibly subsidize exports, prohibit imports, grant supporting contracts, and embed spyware without the WTO and foreign purchasers being any the wiser.

China's State Trading Challenge

China remains a state trading regime in violation of WTO rules in new, more sophisticated forms, permitting enterprise managers to entrepreneurially profit-seek for the Communist Party's benefit. Appearances to the contrary notwithstanding, the Communist Party is fully in command just as it was under Mao Zedong, including the de facto right of rescinding leases at will, and is free to pursue predatory export and import principles harming American workers without detection, just as Trump alleges and elite progressives deny.

The counter-tariffs imposed under Trump's presidency redressed some of the harm caused by China's veiled state trading. They reduced China's enormous trade surplus with the United States (see Table 14.1), but the Biden administration, for diverse reasons, terminated Trump's initiative, substituting restrictions on high-tech microchips and chip technologies that have not worked.

On February 14, 2020, the Economic and Trade Agreement between the United States of America and the People's Republic of China: Phase I went into effect. Under the deal, China agreed to expand purchases of certain United States goods and services by $200 billion for the two-year period January 1, 2020, through December 31, 2021, above 2017 baseline levels.

Table 14.1 reveals why the deal was necessary. It shows that the Chinese Communist Party had a strong preference for running balance of trade surpluses with the United States. China, since joining the WTO, routinely exported four times more than it imported from America,

---

[4] The State-owned Assets Supervision and Administration Commission of the State Council is a special commission of the People's Republic of China, directly under the State Council. It was founded in 2003 through the consolidation of various other industry-specific ministries.

Table 14.1 2000–2020: United States trade in goods with China

Year	Exports	Imports	Balance
2000	16,185.2	100,018.2	−83,833.0
2005	41,192.0	243,470.1	−202,278.1
2010	91,911.1	364,952.6	−273,041.6
2015	115,873.4	483,201.7	−367,328.3
2020	124,485.4	434,749.0	−310,263.5

Note: All figures are in millions of US dollars on a nominal basis, and are not seasonally adjusted unless otherwise specified. Details may not equal totals due to rounding. Table reflects only those months for which there was trade.

Source: United States Census Bureau, https://www.census.gov/foreign-trade/balance/c5700.html

resulting in a huge trade surplus that quintupled between 2000 and 2018 before Trump's countervailing tariffs significantly diminished the imbalance. China's surplus with the United States was $418 billion in 2018. It fell to 310 billion two years later.[5]

Xi has the authority and tools to eliminate the trade surplus. He can use his powers to increase imports from the US, paying for them with government-held foreign exchange reserves. China had $3.2 trillion of reserves as of June 2021. Its officials pretended that market forces were responsible for the trade imbalances, conveniently disregarding the fact that the Communist Party manages exports and imports. Xi could have foregone trade surpluses if this served his purposes.[6] The Biden administration could have pressed him on the matter under Phase I of the US–China Trade Imbalance Reduction Deal. The Peterson Institute for International Economics reported that China's purchases of all covered products reached 62% (Chinese imports) or 60% (US exports) of the Phase I commitment. This was a good start. The Biden administration recognized Trump's accomplishment and initially said that it intended to continue reducing the trade imbalance.

---

[5]United States Census Bureau (2022): Trade balance. https://www.census.gov/foreign-trade/balance/c5700.html
[6]Rosefielde, S. (2012): China's Perplexing Foreign Trade Policy: Causes, Consequences and a Tit for Tat Solution, *American Foreign Policy Interests*, Vol. 33, No. 1, 10–16.

United States Trade Representative Katherine Tai on October 4, 2021 declared the Biden administration's intention to retain United States tariffs on hundreds of billions of dollars of imports from China to press Beijing to honor its Phase I commitment, but Biden never followed through. Even though Xi adapted to American pressure, Washington lacked the resolve to build on partial success, preferring to find excuses for avoiding nudging Beijing on this and other important economic issues. The larger prognosis for Sino–American relations under a Harris presidency is moving forward on a treadmill of procrastination with eyes wide shut. The Democratic Party will not buck its big business supporters for the sake of fair trade, but will impose tariffs to protect "strategic industries."[7] Anti-business progressives will not bite the hand that feeds them.

If Trump wins the November election, he is apt to reinstate counter-sanctions that mitigate the damage inflicted on American workers from unfair Chinese state-subsidized competition.

Chinese Military Challenge

China is a rising superpower striving to replace America as the hegemon of the Asia-Pacific and rival it elsewhere across the globe. It is rapidly increasing the size of its nuclear arsenal,[8] and pressing territorial demands in the South China Sea including Taiwan.[9] A clash of civilizations has begun between an immovable object and an irresistible force. Something must give. Washington has been closely monitoring the challenge for a

---

[7]Lawder, D. (2024): US locks in steep China tariff hikes, many to start Sept. 27. *Reuters*. https://www.reuters.com/markets/us/us-industry-seeks-easing-steep-biden-harris-china-tariff-hikes-2024-08-26/

"The Biden administration on Friday locked in steep tariff hikes on Chinese imports, including a 100% duty on electric vehicles, to strengthen protections for strategic domestic industries from China's state-driven excess production capacity.

"The U.S. Trade Representative's said that many of the tariffs, including a 100% duty on Chinese EVs, 50% on solar cells and 25% on steel, aluminum, EV batteries and key minerals, would go into effect on Sept. 27."

[8]Rajagopalan, R. (2024): China's nuclear forces continue to expand, *The Diplomat*. https://thediplomat.com/2024/01/chinas-nuclear-forces-continue-to-expand/

[9]Rosefielde, S. and Mills, D. (2021): *Beleaguered Superpower: Biden's America Adrift*, Singapore: World Scientific.

Rosefielde, S. (2023): *Russo-Ukrainian War: Implications for the Asia Pacific*, Singapore: World Scientific.

decade. It has "pivoted" its focus to the Asia-Pacific; built alliances with Japan, Australia, New Zealand, and India; and developed the Pacific Air–Sea Battle Plan (Joint Concept for Access and Maneuver in the Global Commons [JAM-GC] strategy), but has done nothing substantive about matching China's arms buildup. As China's navy rapidly increases and its technologies improve, America's fleet continues to shrink,[10] compromising deterrence in Taiwan and the Korean theater, and navigation rights in the South China Sea.[11]

Neither Harris nor Trump have addressed the gap between America's duty to defend, and its unwillingness to spend to assure the nation's security. They will do their best to talk about other issues during the fall campaign. If elected, Trump will try to improve America's military position in the Asia-Pacific. If Kamala wins, she will do nothing.

---

[10] Eaglen, M. (2024): China has built the strongest military in the Indo-Pacific, *AEI*. https://www.aei.org/op-eds/china-has-built-the-strongest-military-in-the-indo-pacific/

"Despite Beijing's publically reported topline of $229 billion in 2022, new research suggests China's real level of military spending was around $711 billion — nearly equal to the U.S. defense budget that same year. … [W]hile China rapidly builds military capacity, the U.S. military is rapidly shrinking across the services. In President Biden's current budget request, the Army will be reduced to just 442,300 active duty soldiers, the smallest it has been since 1940. The U.S. Navy is half the size it was 40 years ago, and set to continue to shrink down to just 294 ships in 2030. At the same time, China's fleet is expected to grow to 425 ships. Similarly, the U.S. Air Force is nearing the smallest it's been since the end of WWII, as retirement of aging aircraft outpaces the purchase of new replacements."

Eaglen, M. (2024): How to break the navy's shipbuilding doom loop. *AEI*. https://www.aei.org/op-eds/how-to-break-the-navys-shipbuilding-doom-loop/

[11] Blumenthal, D., Kagan, F., Turek, A., Shats, D., and Sperzel, M. (2024): Exploring a PRC short-of-war coercion campaign to seize Taiwan's Kinmen Islands and possible responses, *Institute for the Study of War*. https://www.understandingwar.org/backgrounder/exploring-prc-short-war-coercion-campaign-seize-taiwan%E2%80%99s-kinmen-islands-and-possible

Chapter 15

Axis of Iniquity

Subduing Russia, China, and the Sino–Russian Coalition

Washington and the North Atlantic Treaty Organization (NATO) today are committed to winning the Russo–Ukrainian War, if not now, then later. They might accept an "honorable" interim peace, but eventually want to subdue the Kremlin. They aspire to contain China and prevent it from displacing the West as the global hegemon. Washington and NATO are aware that Russia and China are in the process of forming commercial and security coalitions. They are determined to parry this new "axis of iniquity" with economic sanctions and asset impoundment,[1] even if these actions exacerbate polarization and accelerate de-globalization,[2] causing immense economic damage to the West and the rest. They might be willing to achieve the same ends with military means, in doing so avoiding economic complications, but refuse to bear the defense burden.

---

[1] Rosefielde, S. and Bernstam, M. (2024): A new solution to finance Ukraine: A trust fund of Russian assets, *The Hill*. https://thehill.com/opinion/finance/4747246-a-new-solution-to-finance-ukraine-a-trust-fund-of-russian-assets/

Rosefielde, S. and Bernstam, M. (2024): Russo-Ukrainian War: Limits of Western Economic Sanctions, *Acta Oeconomica*, Vol. 74, No. 1, 1–17.

[2] Rosefielde, S. (2025): Impairing Globalization: Western Economic Sanctions and Asset Seizures, *Journal of Risk and Financial Management*, Special Issue on Globalization and Economic Integration.

Sino–Russian Coalition

Vladimir Putin and Xi Jinping have forged a powerful relationship. They have met more than 40 times virtually and in person. In June 2018, Xi described Putin as "an old friend of the Chinese people" and his "best friend."[3] They signed a strong joint statement in Harbin, May 16, 2024 reiterating an early declaration issued in February 2022 portraying their relationship as "superior to political and military alliances of the Cold War era."[4]

A strong Sino–Russian coalition could produce intense gray-zone aggression and anti-Western color revolutions, including, as Putin recently threatened, providing third parties with missiles to strike America and Europe.[5] China today has the world's largest navy.[6] If Xi joins Putin in dispersing long-range strike weapons to insurrectionaries in Latin America and the Middle East, the carnage could be significant.

The Sino–Russian coalition may decide to initiate a joint proxy war against the West. Putin and Xi might persuade Kim Jong Un to assert "just cause," abrogate the Korean Peninsula armistice, and conquer South Korea. Moscow and Beijing can easily supply North Korea with arms,[7] technical personnel, and financing under Biden's Russo–Ukrainian proxy

---

[3] McGovern, R. (2024): Russia & China — Two against one, *Consortium News*. https://consortiumnews.com/2024/05/17/ray-mcgovern-russia-china-two-against-one/

[4] McGovern, R. (2024): Russia & China — Two against one, *Consortium News*. https://consortiumnews.com/2024/05/17/ray-mcgovern-russia-china-two-against-one/

[5] Saksornchai, J. (2024): Southeast Asian diplomats meet with China as friction mounts over Beijing's sweeping maritime claims, *Associated Press News*. https://apnews.com/article/asean-laos-china-america-south-china-sea-9f51f4e931ca34c859113a4d7da79267

[6] As of 2024, it is the second largest navy in the world (behind the United States Navy) in terms of total displacement, and the largest navy per number of ships in active service. https://en.wikipedia.org/wiki/People%27s_Liberation_Army_Navy

[7] Park, J. and Episkopos, M. (2024): Putin and Kim in Pyongyang, making it 'strategic', *Responsible Statecraft*. https://responsiblestatecraft.org/russia-north-korea/

RT. (2024): Russia and North Korea agree on mutual aid against aggression — Putin. https://www.rt.com/news/599552-russia-north-korea-mutual-defense/

Doctorow, G. (2024): Russia will consider dispatch of F16s to Ukraine as aggression that activates its mutual defense agreement with North Korea. https://gilbertdoctorow.com/2024/06/19/russia-will-consider-dispatch-of-f16s-to-ukraine-as-aggression-that-activates-its-mutual-defense-agreement-with-north-korea/

Amar, T. (2024): Seoul searching: Why South Korea has only got itself to blame for having special reasons to worry about Russia's and North Korea's newly elevated cooperation. https://tarikcyrilamar.substack.com/p/seoul-searching

war rules, and then bend redlines by supplying Pyongyang with deep strike missiles.[8]

They can acquire missiles from North Korea for use against Western allies.[9] The United States and NATO, driven to the brink, could be forced to choose between acquiescing to Eastern authoritarian victory or waging World War III.

Economic Sanctions

Economic sanctions are legal injunctions and penalties imposed on offending nations' imports, exports, and assets. The West can restrict trade with Russia and China in varying degrees and can seize their financial assets. Proponents contend that economic sanctions might tame or defeat the "axis of iniquity" by inflicting pain on consumers, reducing China and Russia's gross domestic product (GDP), and denying access to strategic imports. Disgruntled consumers raise the specter of regime change. Diminished GDP increases the defense burden and reduces access to foreign weapons, munitions, critical components, and technologies, which degrades warfighting capability.

The West has sanctioned Russia and China intermittently for more than a century. The latest round of sanctions began in the wake of Russia's annexation of Crimea in 2014, intensified after Russia invaded Ukraine on February 24, 2022, and are still cresting. They caused Russia's GDP to fall by 2.1% in 2022, but its GDP swiftly recovered by 3.5% in 2023, and is currently growing at a 5.3% pace. The Biden administration blames these disappointing results on trade diversion. China, India, Turkey, Iran, and others provided Russia with import substitutes for sanctioned goods, and helped the Kremlin sell its petroleum across the globe.

Cave, D. (2024): Putin came to Asia to disrupt, and he succeeded, *The New York Times*. https://www.nytimes.com/2024/06/22/world/asia/putin-korea-china-disruption.html

Cha, V. and Kim, E. (2024): The new Russia-North Korea security alliance, *Centre for Strategic & International Studies*. https://www.csis.org/analysis/new-russia-north-korea-security-alliance

[8] McCarthy, S. and Chernova, A. (2024): Russia's Putin to visit North Korea in rare trip as anti-West alignment deepens, *CNN*. https://edition.cnn.com/2024/06/17/asia/north-korea-russia-putin-visit-intl-hnk/index.html

[9] Ismay, J. (2024): North Korean missiles rain down on Ukraine despite sanctions, *New York Times*. https://www.nytimes.com/2024/09/11/us/russia-north-korea-missiles-ukraine.html

Washington responded by labeling countries importing and exporting goods it deems essential to sustaining the Russo–Ukrainian proxy war as "enablers."[10] The West now is punishing enablers, particularly China, with secondary sanctions, accomplished by prohibiting alleged violators from settling accounts through the SWIFT (Society for Worldwide Interbank Financial Telecommunications) mechanism.[11]

China and Russia both countered by expanding their own alternative financial clearing mechanisms,[12] and deepening their coalition.

---

[10] Lau, S. (2024): US accuses China of backing Russia's invasion of Ukraine, *Politico*, https://www.politico.eu/article/us-accuses-china-backing-russias-invasion-of-ukraine/

"China is helping Russia meet its war goals in Ukraine by continuing to sell supplies such as drone technology and gunpowder ingredients to Moscow, the U.S. Ambassador to NATO said in an interview." Beijing is providing "machine tools, microelectronics, UAV technologies and nitrocellulose that is used as a propellant."

"Unmanned aerial vehicles (UAVs), more commonly known as drones, have played a significant role in the war for both sides, while China's massive output of nitrocellulose — a key ingredient for making gunpowder — is a concern for Europe's own defense industry.

"Smith said there's no evidence yet of China providing 'lethal support' to Russia, but China is sending equipment and technology that can be used for both civilian and military purposes — and that is helping supply Vladimir Putin's forces."

Sanger, D. (2024): NATO accuses China of supplying Russia's attacks on Ukraine, *The New York Times*. https://www.nytimes.com/2024/07/10/us/politics/nato-china-russia-ukraine.html

Albright, D. and Faragasso, S. (2024): Russian company Elmak procures 'high priority' items for Russia's war efforts via China, *Institute for Science and International Security*. https://isis-online.org/isis-reports/detail/russian-company-elmak-procures-high-priority-items-for-russias-war-efforts

[11] The vast majority of global interbank financial telecommunications transactions are performed by a cooperative called the Society for Worldwide Interbank Financial Telecommunication (SWIFT) established in Belgium in 1973. https://en.wikipedia.org/wiki/SWIFT.

The United States Treasury Department and the European Union monitor transactions and use SWIFT to freeze and impound financial assets of sanctioned private and government entities. SWIFT is the core instrument of the West's economic sanctions mechanism.

Farrell, H. and Newman, A. L. (2019): Weaponized Interdependence: How Global Economic Networks Shape State Coercion, *International Security*, Vol. 44, No. 1, 42–79.

[12] China, Russia, and India, fearing Western economic sanctions, have developed substitutes. China's surrogate is the Cross-border Interbank Payment System (CIPS). It offers clearing and settlement services for its participants in cross-border renminbi (RMB)

Western action aimed at freezing and potentially impounding $300 billion of Russian financial assets to finance Ukraine is polarizing East–West relations further.[13] China with just cause is apprehensive that the West may confiscate its financial assets in the same manner.

The net result of sanctions on Russia, China, and the Sino–Russian coalition, including financial asset seizures on Russia, has been adverse. On one hand, they have not crushed Russia and China's GDPs, prompted regime change, compelled a favorable settlement of the Russo–Ukrainian War, or provided any sign that the West is likely to permanently eradicate the Sino–Russian coalition threat. On the other, they have accelerated de-dollarization bypassing SWIFT, facilitated trade diversion through coalition networks, prompted China to consider selling hundreds of billion dollars of United States Treasury securities, alerted the Global South to reduce business with the West, and spawned de-globalization by warping and diminishing world trade.[14] The Russian and Chinese economic systems are more powerful than Washington is willing to contemplate.[15]

America's ambition to remain global hegemon without acquiring the requisite military power by means of economic sanctions and asset

---

payments and trade. CIPS is backed by the People's Bank of China and was launched in 2015 as part of a policy effort to internationalize the use of China's currency. It covers more than 4,200 banking institutions in 182 countries and regions around the world. In 2022, CIPS processed around 96.7 trillion yuan ($14.03 trillion), with about 1,427 financial institutions in 109 countries and regions having connected to the system. Russia banned SWIFT on 20 March 2023 for banking transactions. Its substitute clearing system is called the System for Transfer of Financial Messages. The system serves 20 states and 550 organizations.

[13] Rosefielde, S. and Bernstam, M. (2024): Proposing the 'Russian trust fund for Ukraine', *The Hill*. https://thehill.com/opinion/finance/4424451-proposing-the-russian-trust-fund-for-ukraine/

[14] Corbin, M. (2024): How far can a Putin-Modi hug go? *Responsible Statecraft*. https://responsiblestatecraft.org/modi-putin-visit/

Rosefielde, S. (2024): Impairing Globalization: Western Economic Sanctions and Asset Seizures, *Journal of Risk and Financial Management (JRFM)*. https://www.mdpi.com/1911-8074/17/9/402/pdf

[15] Heath, T., Reach, C., and Mazarr, M. (2024): The societal basis for national competitiveness, *Rand*. https://www.rand.org/content/dam/rand/pubs/research_reports/RRA2600/RRA2611-1/RAND_RRA2611-1.pdf

impoundment appears misconceived and apt to backfire economically and strategically.

Neither Kamala Harris nor Donald Trump appears to have an inkling of the danger.

If they ever comprehend the complex forces shaping the West's future, Harris will simply deny what is visible in plain sight, and Trump will try to cut a deal because he has never been an advocate of strategic economic sanctions and does not share the establishment view that Russia is diabolic and China incorrigible. He would choose prosperity over power.

Chapter 16

Hamas–Israeli War

Yahya Sinwar, leader of Hamas in the Gaza Strip, launched a surprise attack against Israel on October 7, 2023 to conquer the Jewish state, establish Hamas rule, expel Jews, and return the land to the Palestinian people, a goal shared by the Democratic Party's anti-colonialist left, but rejected by Joe Biden and Republicans. The Democrats have long advocated for a two-state solution requiring Israel to establish an independent Palestinian authority in Gaza and the West Bank, territories conquered by Israel in 1972 after Egypt, Syria, and Jordan lost the Yom Kippur War. Israel agreed to the two-state formula, but could not conclude the process with an unstable and undemocratic Palestinian authority, led first by terrorist group Fatah, and then Hamas.

Hamas is the Sunni Islamist political and military organization that rules the Gaza Strip. The United States designated Sinwar and Hamas as "terrorists" in September 2015.

Sinwar's strategy is to create a permanent crisis by crying genocide, playing on global anti-Semitic and anti-colonialist sentiment to isolate and weaken Israel for the final kill. He talks about a ceasefire and peaceful reconciliation, but it means Israel's unconditional surrender. This has created a quagmire for the Biden administration that seeks to placate the Democratic Party's anti-colonialist left, without alienating Israel's domestic American supporters. It has chosen to manage the problem by double-speaking, allowing the progressive media of record to rail against Israeli genocide without sanctioning Tel Aviv, while simultaneously sponsoring peace talks and providing humanitarian assistance to the Palestinians. As the November presidential election nears, Biden curbed the media's hyperbolic genocide rhetoric, denounced anti-Semitism, quietly pressured universities to restrain Palestinian activists, and tilted toward supporting Israel's right to self-defense.

Nonetheless, the disparity between Kamala Harris and Donald Trump on resolving the Hamas–Israeli conflict is immense. Trump is ardently pro-Israeli. Harris leans toward the anti-colonialist pro-Palestinian position, even though in the Harris–Trump debate on September 10, 2024 she pledged to defend Israel's right to exist.[1]

Often describing himself as the "best friend that Israel has ever had,"[2] Trump claims that, if he had been president, Hamas' attack would have been averted. He promises to cut off US aid to Palestinians and keep Israel safe, asserting that "Nobody else will, nobody else can."[3] He pledged to avoid rewarding Hamas for aggression with American assistance in rebuilding postwar Gaza, and asserted that he will bar Palestinian refugees and foreign nationals advocating for Israel's eradication. Trump promises to expel immigrants who sympathize with Hamas and to revoke the visas of anti-American and anti-Semitic foreign students.

He hopes that his staunch commitment to Israel and opposition to violent anti-Israeli and anti-Semitic demonstrations supported by Democratic Party progressives will attract Jewish voters to the Republican Party.

Trump's campaign spokesperson Karoline Levitt, restating his position with the intention of prodding Jewish votes to abandon the Democratic Party, said that "Jewish Americans are realizing that the Democrat party has turned into a full-blown anti-Israel, anti-Semitic, pro-terrorist cabal, and that's why more and more Jewish Americans are supporting President Trump."[4] This message reverberates with evangelical Christians, strengthening their commitment to Trump.

---

[1] Riesman, J. and Rosenbaum, S. (2024): Kamala is sending a subtle message on Israel. Is anyone listening? *Slate*. https://slate.com/news-and-politics/2024/09/kamala-harris-israel-policy-palestine-gaza-war.html

[2] Gambino, L. (2024): What would Trump's Israel-Gaza policy be if he were re-elected? *The Guardian*. https://www.theguardian.com/us-news/2024/apr/25/trump-presidency-israel-gaza-middle-east-crisis

[3] Gambino, L. (2024): What would Trump's Israel-Gaza policy be if he were re-elected? *The Guardian*. https://www.theguardian.com/us-news/2024/apr/25/trump-presidency-israel-gaza-middle-east-crisis

[4] Gambino, L. (2024): What would Trump's Israel-Gaza policy be if he were re-elected? *The Guardian*. https://www.theguardian.com/us-news/2024/apr/25/trump-presidency-israel-gaza-middle-east-crisis

Trump's pro-Israel posture is genuine. It echoes his presidential policy initiatives in 2016–2020. During his term as president, he moved the US embassy from Tel Aviv to Jerusalem, recognized Israel's sovereignty over the Golan Heights, slashed funding to the United Nations agency supporting Palestinian refugees, and closed the Palestinians' diplomatic mission in Washington.

He withdrew the US from the Iran nuclear deal, viewed by many as stealthily assisting Teheran's acquisition of nuclear weapons, disclaimers to the contrary notwithstanding, and declared in 2019 that America no longer considered Israeli settlements in the West Bank a violation of international law.

Trump's biggest accomplishment in the Middle East was the Abraham accords, normalizing diplomatic relations among Israel, the United Arab Emirates, and Bahrain.

If Trump wins the election, he will restore United States approval of Israeli settlements in the West Bank and suppress pro-Palestinian instigation of anti-semitism on American university campuses.[5]

Harris opposes all of Trump's promises and pledges regarding Israel and the Palestinians. She is committed to the Biden administration's Middle East double-think and double-speak on all aspects of the issue.

If push comes to shove, Harris will accommodate the pro-Palestinian left within the Democratic Party. She will press Israel to accommodate Yahya Sinwar's insincere assurances of benign intent, despite his malign endgame.

---

[5] Gambino, L. (2024): What would Trump's Israel-Gaza policy be if he were re-elected? *The Guardian.* https://www.theguardian.com/us-news/2024/apr/25/trump-presidency-israel-gaza-middle-east-crisis

Chapter 17

Iran

Iran has been a thorn in America's side since the 1979 Islamic Revolution brought Ayatollah Khomeini to power as Supreme Leader, leading to the creation of an Islamic republic. He backed Shia militancy to combat Sunni influence and establish Iranian Muslim dominance, closing all universities in Iran until 1983. The United States and Iran severed diplomatic relations in April 1980. The United States classified Iran as a State Sponsor of Terrorism in 1984 for support given to Hezbollah, Palestinian terrorist groups in Gaza, and various terrorist and militant groups in Iraq, Syria, Bahrain, and elsewhere throughout the Middle East.[1] The Islamic Revolutionary Guard Corp, a multi-service primary branch of the Iranian Armed Forces, has been key to Iranian influence through its Quds Force specializing in unconventional warfare and military intelligence operations.

The 2005 presidential election brought conservative populist and nationalist candidate Mahmoud Ahmadinejad to power. He promoted nuclear development, and aggression against Israel, Saudi Arabia, the United Kingdom, and the United States.

President Hassan Rouhani supported the Joint Comprehensive Plan of Action (JCPOA) reached in Vienna in 2015, between Iran, the P5+1 (United Nations Security Council + Germany), and the European Union, centered around ending the economic sanctions in exchange for Iran restricting enriched uranium production. The Trump administration

---

[1] U.S Department of State (2024): Country reports on terrorism 2021: Iran. https://www.state.gov/reports/country-reports-on-terrorism-2021/iran/

determined that Iran's assurances were inadequate, and sanctions relief unjustified. America withdrew from the deal and new sanctions were imposed. In August 2023, President Joe Biden allowed Tehran access to some $6 billion (€5.58 billion) in oil assets frozen in South Korea in exchange for the release of five United States hostages held in Iran. In March 2024, he allowed Iran access to another $10 billion in frozen assets, perpetuating the Democratic Party's solicitous attitude toward Iran, despite its designation by the United States Department of State as a State Sponsor of Terrorism.[2]

Whatever Washington's motives, its efforts to woo Tehran have not yielded tangible benefits. Iran energetically contests America's allies in the Middle East and supports the Kremlin militarily and economically in the Russo–Ukrainian War.[3]

It is a Russian enabler. Tehran is sending Kremlin drones and ballistic missiles,[4] and is energetically assisting Moscow in evading Western economic sanctions.[5] It is also an enabler of the Houthis, a Zaydi Shiite movement fighting Yemen's Sunni government since 2004.[6] In Syria, Iran has supported America's adversary, President Bashar al-Assad. It has

---

[2] Sayeh, J., Taleblu, B., and Ghasseminejad, S. (2024): Why the Biden Administration's Iran sanctions waivers are futile, *Foundation for Defense of Democracies*. https://www.fdd.org/analysis/2024/05/10/why-the-biden-administrations-iran-sanctions-waivers-are-futile/

Wall Street Journal Editorial Board. (2024): Biden gives Iran another sanctions break. https://www.wsj.com/articles/biden-administration-iran-sanctions-waiver-israel-elor-azaria-b86bec8f

[3] Lopez, C. (2024): Iran gives Russia short-range missiles, while U.S. partners expect to keep bolstering Ukrainian air defense, *U.S. Department of Defense*. https://www.defense.gov/News/News-Stories/Article/Article/3901774/iran-gives-russia-short-range-missiles-while-us-partners-expect-to-keep-bolster/

Geranmayeh, E. and Grajewski, N. (2024): Alone together: How the war in Ukraine shapes the Russian-Iranian relationship, *European Council on Foreign Relations*. https://ecfr.eu/publication/alone-together-how-the-war-in-ukraine-shapes-the-russian-iranian-relationship/

[4] Hafezi, P., Irish, J., Balmforth, T., and Landay, J. (2024): Exclusive: Iran sends Russia hundreds of ballistic missiles, *Reuters*. https://www.reuters.com/world/iran-sends-russia-hundreds-ballistic-missiles-sources-say-2024-02-21/

[5] Kohlmann, T. (2024): Why Iran and Russia can dodge Western sanctions, *DW News*. https://www.dw.com/en/why-iran-and-russia-can-dodge-western-sanctions/a-68928255

[6] Robinson, K. (2024): Iran's support of the Houthis: What to know, *Council on Foreign Relations*. https://www.cfr.org/in-brief/irans-support-houthis-what-know

embraced Hamas to undermine the popularity of the Palestine Liberation Organization.

Tehran aspires to be an anti-American, nuclear, terrorist, Shiite Islamic regional hegemon, dominating Iraq, Saudi Arabia, Yemen, Qatar, the United Arab Emirates, Syria, Lebanon, Kurdistan, and Turkey.

Democratic Party progressives find this inspiring. They defend Tehran with specious justifications without revealing their hidden agendas.

If Kamala Harris becomes president, she will continue coddling Iran. Her campaign is already chastising Donald Trump for withdrawing from the JCPOA,[7] falsely attributing Iran's nuclear development to the rejection of the Democrats' agreement.

If Trump becomes president, he will take a firm line to Iran's transgressions, especially regarding economic sanctions.[8]

---

[7] Hein, S. (2024): US election: How would Kamala Harris deal with Iran? *DW News*. https://www.dw.com/en/us-election-how-would-kamala-harris-deal-with-iran/a-69764798

[8] Iran. (2024): Trump and Harris clash over Iran and Israel in presidential debate. https://www.iranintl.com/en/202409110120

Chapter 18

Cuba

An immigration crisis from 2021 to 2023 ravaged Cuba. An estimated 500,000 Cubans sought refuge in the United States in this period, accounting for nearly 5% of Cuba's population. Three hundred thousand Cuban refugees settled in Miami-Dade County. The mass exodus, prompted by economic hardships and political uncertainties, has posed humanitarian, social, and political challenges for both Cuba and the United States, prompting discussions and negotiations between the two nations to manage the flow of migrants. The emigrant flight caught progressives off guard, but they should not have been surprised. You do not need a weatherman to know which way the wind is blowing. The migration crisis is only the most recent example of Cuban revolutionary socialist failure.

Fidel Castro's guerilla army defeated Cuban President Fulgencio Batista's military dictatorship on December 31, 1958. He installed a Marxist-Leninist one-party socialist dictatorship (Republic of Cuba) the next day. Castro canceled capitalism; abolishing private property, criminalizing markets and entrepreneurship, and compelling the able-bodied workforce to toil in state-owned enterprises or agricultural cooperatives. The economy during these early years was a centrally planned command regime with wages and prices fixed by the state price committee. The Communist Party ruled as it thought best on behalf of the workers, imposing appropriate economic, legal, political, and social institutions. This mainly involved state price-fixing, a state foreign-trade monopoly, central planning, state enterprise management, rationing, subsidized services, free universal education, and criminalization of markets. Castro was committed to communist egalitarianism. He imposed income, status, ethnic, and gender equality, and suppressed class enemies.

The Marxist logic of state control and egalitarianism drove Castro's revolutionary communist policies. He transferred assets confiscated from private owners to the state's account and provided basic housing, transport, medical, educational services, food, and other necessities to the masses. He re-trained, redeployed, and expanded the labor force to meet revolutionary objectives. Castro exhorted women and minorities to work outside their homes, receiving equal pay for equal work. The Cuban Republic granted them equal access to education and occupational opportunities. All these confiscatory and redistributive actions benefited the workers and peasants, but had deficiencies. The Cuban Communist Party decided where people worked, occupations, terms of labor, and the amount and assortment of goods produced and rationed. Castro compelled Cubans to work and rationed jobs, higher educational opportunities, and consumption, straitjacketing their entrepreneurial initiative and personal freedom. Workers and peasants had some small voice, but their elite leaders illiberally compelled them to obey. Although Castro had been optimistic, disappointing results prompted him to consider other options.

He gravitated toward Deng Xiaoping's marketization strategy of "crossing the river by feeling the stones" (1980–1997).[1] Castro permitted a small number of workers to operate as private entrepreneurs in the early 1990s, and legalized small private business more broadly in 2016, but stopped short of Xi Jinping's leasehold entrepreneurial market communism. The private sector gradually grew from 1994 to 2021. Private enterprises today employ approximately a quarter of the labor force, but results have been lackluster.

The performance of Cuba's mixed plan and market reform model after 1994 should have paralleled Deng's achievements, but Castro's model underperformed. Cuba failed to develop effective market transition institutions like Deng's "town-village-enterprises" (TVEs) in the second mixed-economy phase.[2]

---

[1] Keo, B. (2024): Crossing the river by feeling the stones: Deng Xiaoping in the making of modern China, *Association for Asian Studies*. https://www.asianstudies.org/publications/eaa/archives/crossing-the-river-by-feeling-the-stones-deng-xiaoping-in-the-making-of-modern-china/

[2] The reforms of 1978 changed TVEs, which became the most vibrant part of the Chinese economy as they experienced significant expansion in the 1980s and early 1990s. TVE employment grew from 28 million in 1978 to a peak of 135 million in 1996.

Castro, like radical American progressives, placed his faith primarily in revolutionary moral fervor and rationing rather than in planning and material incentives before 1994, and continued to do so afterwards under the Cuban mixed command-market regime. Although Fidel, and later Raul Castro,[3] could have emulated the Chinese market communist mechanism, they chose a hybrid Maoist–New Economic Policy model.[4]

This preference for relying on redness more than material incentives, expert planning, and for-profit management distinguishes Cuba from Soviet communism. Joseph Stalin and Castro both employed redness (the criminalization of private property, markets and entrepreneurship, and revolutionary zeal and terror) to construct their socialist orders, but Castro under-weighted central planning.[5] The Soviets prioritized superpower, while Castro emphasized redness in the economic and social spheres at the expense of prosperity. The Soviet Union successfully industrialized and became a military superpower, while Cuba did neither.

The subpar economic performance of Cuban Marxist-Leninism judged from its revolutionary promises and the Soviet–Chinese benchmarks is most likely attributable to Castro's prioritization of redness over expertness and liberalization. The Soviet and Cuban models both were straitjacket economies of shortage and rationing that allowed leaders to boast about ostensible ideological benefits of proletarian liberation, but the Soviet and later Xi Jinping variant delivered much more.[6]

Naughton, B. (2017): *The Chinese Economy: Transitions and Growth*, Cambridge: MIT Press.

[3] Raul Castro was First Secretary of the Communist Party of Cuba (2011–2021).

[4] Cheng, Y. (2007): Fidel Castro and "China's Lesson for Cuba": A Chinese Perspective, *The China Quarterly*, No. 189, 24–42.

Cheng, Y. (2012): The "Socialist Other": Cuba in Chinese Ideological Debates Since the 1990s, *The China Quarterly*, No. 209, 198–216.

González-Corzo, M. (2012): Entrepreneurship in Transition Economies: Selected Characteristics and Relevant Lessons for the Future of Cuba, *Journal of Current Chinese Affairs*, Vol. 41, No. 1, 155–179.

[5] According to the "Black Book of Communism," death squads had shot at least 14,000 Cubans by 1970s; in all, more than 100,000 have died or been killed as a result of the revolution. In 1960, Cuba established its first gulag-style concentration camps.

Courtois, S. and Margolin, J. et al. (1999): *The Black Book of Communism: Crimes, Terror, Repression*, Cambridge MA: Harvard University Press.

[6] Naím, M. and Toro, F. (2020): Venezuela's problem isn't Socialism: Maduro's mess has little to do with ideology, *Carnegie Endowment for International Peace*. https://carnegieendowment.org/2020/01/27/venezuela-s-problem-isn-t-socialism-pub-80909

Cuba's over-dependence on redness, like similar revolutionary progressive promises today, was a trap. Castro's strategy for success was a wager on egalitarian politics, and blind faith that the nationalization of wealth, equal income, status, and opportunity would magically provide workers with a high quality of existence, when in practice his revolutionary egalitarian politics camouflaged inequities, depressed living standards, and repressed personal freedom. Red revolutionary communist regimes eschew initiative for private benefit and ration supplies. Workers cannot improve themselves for personal benefit and reserve their effort. They are disempowered and at the Communist Party's mercy. If officials abuse their authority, workers have no recourse against the one-party state. There is no escape from red revolutionary triumphalism.[7]

This reality is easily illustrated. Most Cubans cannot afford to purchase unsubsidized goods in state and private retail outlets. They subsist on approximately US$200 per year.[8] The state owns the housing stock but under-maintains it. Communist Party insiders receive the best apartments. Women hold seemingly prestigious positions in the medical profession but receive the average state salary. Women have little influence in the Communist Party, holding only 7% of the powerful positions. Machismo is rampant, and racial discrimination is acute. Black women receive the lowest-paying jobs and have the highest rates of unemployment and the lowest education levels. They often live with the threat of gender violence. Cuba has imitators. None succeeded.

Kamala Harris will not concede that Cuba is a failed socialist experiment, and that the 2021–2023 immigration crisis will strengthen Donald Trump's support in Florida. Elite progressives have not betrayed the egalitarian and anti-meritocratic faith for more than a half century. They will not admit error now, nor alter course. Trump will stress the point in Florida and to other sympathetic Hispanic communities. Many will pay attention.

---

[7] Torpor is a state of decreased physiological activity in an animal, usually by a reduced body temperature and metabolic rate. Torpor enables animals to survive periods of reduced food availability.

[8] CODEPINK (2015): Dividing the pie: Cuba's ration system after 50 years. https://www.codepink.org/dividing_the_pie_cuba_s_ration_system_after_50_years

Chapter 19

Venezuela

President Hugo Chávez launched an elite left-wing populist Bolivarian Revolution in 1999 to build democracy, economic independence, achieve an equitable distribution of income, and end political corruption, culminating in the Fifth Republic of Venezuela. He squandered the nation's oil wealth, transforming Venezuela from one of the richest countries in Latin America to one of the poorest, precipitating the largest emigration of people in Latin America's history. Over seven million refugees, approximately 20% of the population, emigrated.

Chavez picked Nicolás Maduro as his successor in 2013 to head the United Socialist Party of Venezuela. Since February 2014, hundreds of thousands have protested over high government-generated levels of criminal violence, corruption, hyperinflation, and chronic scarcity of basic goods. The government began taking more money from PDVSA (Petróleos de Venezuela, S.A.), the state oil company, discouraging oil field reinvestment. Production decreased from three to one million barrels per day in 2014.

Maduro won a contested and controversial second presidential term on January 10, 2019. His Supreme Tribunal, which had been overturning National Assembly decisions since the opposition took control, usurped the functions of the assembly, and created the 2017 Venezuelan constitutional crisis. In December 2017, Maduro barred opposition parties after they boycotted mayoral polls in 2018. The Trump administration imposed an economic embargo against Venezuela in 2019, and the next year indicted Maduro on charges of drug trafficking, narcoterrorism, and corruption.

The Biden administration subsequently reached an understanding with the Maduro regime, lifting Donald Trump's sanctions on oil and gas in return for steps toward free and fair presidential elections, but reimposed them again in April 2024 because Maduro failed to fulfill his promises.[1]

On July 29, 2024, the Venezuelan government announced that Maduro had been re-elected president. United States Secretary of State Antony Blinken said that the United States had "serious concerns that the result announced does not reflect the will or the voters of the Venezuelan people."[2] He is undoubtedly correct.

The Biden administration's Venezuela strategy is in shambles. Prospects for the democratic opposition are bleak.[3] America's indulgent attitude toward Venezuela's left-wing populist Bolivarian Revolution failed to transform the nation into a progressive showcase. The egalitarian revolutionary tactics that Democratic Party progressives earnestly advocate extinquished individual, social, political, and economic liberty and impoverished a once prosperous people.

Trump will surely remind Kamala Harris that he told Democratic Party progressives indulging Maduro's United Socialist Party of Venezuela that this would happen. Harris will duck and cover.

---

[1] Otis, J. (2024): Biden reinstates sanctions on Venezuela, *National Public Radio*. https://www.npr.org/2024/04/18/1245650630/biden-reinstates-sanctions-on-venezuela

[2] Cano, R. and Goodman, J. (2024): Maduro is declared winner in Venezuela's presidential election as opposition claims it prevailed, *AP News*. https://apnews.com/article/venezuela-presidential-election-maduro-machado-edmundo-5ce255ae90614162590bfe1207d2e1d0

[3] Phillips, T. (2024): Is it game over for Venezuela's opposition as Maduro clings to power? *Guardian*. https://www.theguardian.com/world/article/2024/sep/11/venezuela-election-maduro-gonzalez-exiled

Chapter 20

World Order

The world today across the economic, social, and political spectrum appears to be degenerating into mayhem. Acute conflict has spurred calls for universal order, both ideal and pragmatic. There is no shortage of utopian, dystopian, and practical suggestions. Communists, socialists, progressives, liberals, populists, revivalists, and technocrats all claim to be the solution, but there is no consensus because utopia for some is dystopia for others, and practical schemes seldom are neutral. Washington has the answer — obey its whims. But Russia, China, North Korea, and the Global South reject America's terms of endearment, and Western progressives are loath to participate in crafting a transnational consensus. They believe that there is no fortress the Bolsheviks cannot storm, meaning that they can have it all. They are mistaken. The West beguiled Russia into suspending its disbelief that Washington was willing to be an accommodative partner for peace. It will not be able to fool the Kremlin again, nor sweet talk China. Even if progressives bamboozle the Muslim world into abandoning Islam, cloning the elite secular ideal, the results will create as many problems as they alleviate. Enmities in the Middle East run deep.

World order in the 21st pluralist century requires tolerantly and patiently building consensus with structurally neutral institutions. Consensus is more than compromise. It entails accepting the validity of other people's concerns and working together with them to find satisficing solutions that improve collective wellbeing.

Many non-partisan scholars grasp that the East, West, and Global South should construct a mutually accommodative consensus building world order.[1] They perceive that the Global South is rising but politicians are not ready for comprehensive, mutually satisfactory power sharing. They are acculturated to shun accommodation, expecting that they will prevail if they try hard enough, and fearing that concessions are tantamount to appeasement. There are a few cultures like Japan's capable of balancing the countervailing pulls of winner-take-all rivalry and mutual accommodation.[2] The West ignores them and its politics are becoming increasingly confrontational.

The "second best" solution, absent consensus, is compromise. Half a loaf is better than none. Joe Biden could have averted the Russo–Ukrainian War in January 2021 by assuring Russian Foreign Minister Sergei Lavrov that Ukraine would never be invited to join the North Atlantic Treaty Organization in return for concessions on Russia's management of Luhansk and Donetsk.

The "third best" solution if all parties are intransigent is to pursue the good and forget the best. Russia and West can contain the scale of the Russo–Ukrainian War and de-escalate, rediscovering the virtue of mutual assured destruction (no brinkmanship, no thermonuclear war).

This entails elevating Spinosa (tolerance) over Rousseau (inalienable rights); creating a global culture that prioritizes tolerance, empathy, consensus, and accommodation, because these values offer a better path than militant self-righteousness.

Embrace a wisdom culture. Discard Nietzsche.

Kamala Harris does not see the light. World Order for her means global left-wing progressivism. This is the path she will plod, if elected. It will exacerbate global polarization, disorder, and increase the risk of a third world war.

Donald Trump does not see the light, but he is stumbling in the right direction.

---

[1] Mahbubani, K. (2013): *The Great Convergence: Asia, the West, and the Logic of One World*. New York: Public Affairs.

[2] Roseflelde, S. (2023): *Socialist Economic Systems: 21st Century Pathways*. New York: Routledge, Chapter 21 (Japanese Communalist Socialism).

Chapter 21

Entangling Treaties

Enlightenment tolerance inspired the American constitution and Bill of Rights.

George Washington grasped that wisdom was the better part of valor and cautioned against entangling alliances in his farewell address. If elite progressives remember the admonition, they disregard it to the nation's detriment.

It seems that the establishment does not understand the concept of optimizing under constraint, preferring to commit America to myriads of entanglements and expecting to muddle through successfully.

Alliances can bolster national security and are not bad in and of themselves. Their merit depends on various pluses and minuses. They can facilitate deterrence and war winning on the plus side, and have the opposite effect on the minus side. Leaders should avoid foolish alliances that subtract value. This includes any alliance that overstretches national resources, even if otherwise beneficial. Alliances are only meritorious if they enhance the quality of national existence in the big picture, given priorities (the objective function) and taking full account of resource constrained opportunity costs.

America's alliance system is defective because its ends exceed the means that the establishment is willing to fund. The system is overextended and detrimentally entangled. It cannot efficiently achieve its goals in the best case and performs poorly in practice, because it finds itself ensnared in unwise entangling commitments.

America may forge an alliance with Israel to fight terrorism but may not want to wage war against Iran on Jerusalem's behalf. The United

States has committed itself to assisting Ukraine reconquer Luhansk, Donetsk, and Crimea, but does not desire to fight a nuclear war to satisfy Kyiv. Felicitous alliances too easily degenerate into traps.

Alliances are also ensnaring because they provide a pretext for mission creep. They foster "bigger is better" rationalizations for costly and dangerous expansions of infrastructure and warfighting commitments.

America's inclination to expand alliances in tandem with economic sanctions is exacerbating catastrophic national security risks. George Washington was prescient.

The establishment does not perceive the danger. It is content with its delusions.[1]

---

[1] Pozen, B. (2016): The high costs and limited benefits of America's alliances, *National Interest*. https://nationalinterest.org/blog/the-skeptics/the-high-costs-limited-benefits-americas-alliances-17273

Bandow, D. (2024): Will Americans stop trying to 'run the world'? Harris and Trump should drop Biden's disastrous grandiosity, *The American Conservative*. https://www.theamericanconservative.com/will-americans-stop-trying-to-run-the-world/

Part VI

Prospects

Chapter 22

Reckless Endangerment

America's progressive establishment elite is herding the nation toward an anti-working class version of revolutionary Cuban socialism and Venezuelan left-wing populism domestically, and destructive forever wars and nuclear brinkmanship abroad.[1] Both policies are irresponsible from the perspective of the West and world's quality of existence, but enthralled by revolutionary power culture, progressives see only fair skies ahead.

Progressives believe that they can beneficently control everything without risking pandemonium despite ubiquitous evidence to the contrary, including immigration crises and wars Washington felt certain it would win but are being lost.[2] They conflate the semblances of their rhetoric with the real consequences of their actions.

Once upon a time, Western intellectuals grasped the importance of Aristotle's "golden mean."[3] This is no longer true. Electoral power

---

[1] Aris, B. (2024): Are we on the cusp of WWIII? *Intellinews*. https://www.intellinews.com/moscow-blog-are-we-on-the-cusp-of-wwiii-343336/?source=blogs

[2] Davies, D. (2024): *The Unaccountability Machine: Why Big Systems Make Terrible Decisions — and How the World Lost its Mind*, New York: Profile Books.

[3] The golden mean is an approach to ethics that emphasizes finding the appropriate medium, or middle ground, between extremes. The phrase golden mean is most frequently applied to the ethical ideas described by the ancient Greek philosopher Aristotle (384–322 BCE) in his treatise *Nicomachean Ethics*. Similar ideas can be found in many cultures, notably in the teachings of Jewish scholar Moses Maimonides, in the "middle way" principle found in Buddhist philosophy, and in the "doctrine of the mean," or *zhongyong*, in Confucianism.

seeking and ideology today have made winning more important than wisdom and the quality of existence. Winning for America's establishment is tantamount to fulfilling impossible dreams, shielding progressives from self-criticism, and critical rational policy assessments.

Their self-delusion is not unique. The Bolsheviks succumbed to it during "war communism" with catastrophic consequences.[4] Mikhail Gorbachev foisted ill-conceived radical reforms on the Soviet Union on July 1, 1987. They destroyed the Union of Soviet Socialist Republics on December 25, 1991.[5]

Vladimir Lenin reversed the Bolshevik's starry-eyed revolutionary course in 1921,[6] but only after industrial production fell 67% and millions died of starvation.[7]

Fidel Castro led Cuba up a blind alley in 1959. It is still wandering in the wilderness.

America's left-wing progressive establishment is guilty of reckless endangerment, even though it is heresy to say so.

Kamala Harris is steeped in the power cult of infantile leftism.[8]

Trump populism has its own pitfalls, but they do not entail reckless endangerment. Populists may overshoot the mark in reversing progressive excesses, but will not wreck the economy, mire the West in forever wars, and risk nuclear annihilation.

---

[4]Nove, A. (1982): *An Economic History of the U.S.S.R.*, Harmondsworth, Middlesex, England: Penguin.

Bukharin, N. and Preobrazhensky, E. (1920): The ABC of Communism. https://www.marxists.org/archive/bukharin/works/1920/abc/index.htm

[5]Rosefielde, S. (2023): *Socialist Economic Systems: 21st Century Pathways*, London: Routledge.

[6]Lenin, V (1917): State and Revolution. https://www.marxists.org/archive/lenin/works/1917/staterev/

Bukharin, N. and Preobrazhensky, E. (1920): ABC of Communism. https://www.marxists.org/archive/bukharin/works/1920/abc/index.htm

[7]Nove, A. (1982): *An Economic History of the U.S.S.R.*, Harmondsworth, Middlesex, England: Penguin.

[8]Lenin, V. (1920): Left-Wing Communism — An Infantile Disorder. https://www.marxists.org/archive/lenin/works/cw/pdf/lenin-cw-vol-31.pdf

Chapter 23

The Election That could Change the World

Scott Ritter, a perceptive arms control and disarmament expert, contends that the United States is on track for a major existential crisis with Russia some time in 2026.[1] Escalation may be occurring faster than he assumes.[2]

He asserts further that "the choices couldn't be starker — the living embodiment of 'DEI establishment politician' (Harris) versus the textbook definition of a 'populist political outsider' (Trump),"[3] implying that the risk of nuclear war with Russia (and China) is linked to the debilitating effects of leftist progressive domestic policy (unwillingness to adequately fund military deterrence), dyspeptic economy, and social polarization.[4]

Right again, but his framing overlooks the possibility that even if the West wins the Russo–Ukrainian proxy war tomorrow, progressive domestic politics is nudging America toward the Cuban and Venezuelan morass.

---

[1] Ritter, S. (2024): Voting against nuclear war, *Consortium News*. https://consortiumnews.com/2024/07/29/scott-ritter-voting-against-nuclear-war/
[2] Jakes, L. (2024): Should Ukraine launch Western weapons deep into Russia? *New York Times*. https://www.nytimes.com/2024/09/12/world/europe/biden-ukraine-strike-russia.html
[3] Ritter, S. (2024): Voting against nuclear war, *Consortium News*. https://consortiumnews.com/2024/07/29/scott-ritter-voting-against-nuclear-war/
[4] Heath, T., Reach, C., and Mazarr, M. (2024): The societal basis for national competitiveness, *Rand*. https://www.rand.org/content/dam/rand/pubs/research_reports/RRA2600/RRA2611-1/RAND_RRA2611-1.pdf

The 2024 American presidential election, therefore, is doubly "existential." The hinge of fate is determining both domestic and international pathways.[5]

Ritter is pessimistic. He contends that "a future Harris administration is on track to continue a policy which commits to the strategic defeat of Russia, the lowering of the threshold for the use of nuclear weapons in Europe, the termination of the last remaining arms control treaty (New START) in February 2026, and the re-deployment of intermediate-range missiles into Europe, also in 2026."

He appreciates that Trump is receptive to opening the door to better relations with Russia, but is not convinced because "the harsh reality is that regardless of who among the two major candidates wins in November, American policy vis-à-vis Russia, especially when it comes to nuclear posture and arms control, is hard-wired to achieve the same result."[6]

Maybe.

Foreign relations are only half the story. America and the world may survive nuclear brinkmanship, but still impoverish itself if Kamala Harris wins. The reprieve Cubans and Venezuelans achieved fleeing their red progressive and socialist paradises may only be temporary.

The 2024 presidential election is apt to be existential in the final analysis because when faced with a choice between the utopian economic delusion and pragmatic moderation, the American electorate may opt for poverty, civil strife, and forever wars instead of moderate reform. The election could also be existential, if voters re-empower a working class that prioritizes prosperity and global consensus building over anti-meritocracy and American hegemony. A Trump victory does not assure the abandonment of the establishment post-World War II conception of world order, but the wind seems to be blowing in this direction.

---

[5] Churchill, W. (1950): *The Hinge of Fate*. New York: Houghton Mifflin.
[6] Ritter, S. (2024): Voting against nuclear war, *Consortium News*. https://consortiumnews.com/2024/07/29/scott-ritter-voting-against-nuclear-war/

Conclusion

Deceptive polarizing slogans obliquely connected with a host of fundamental problems besetting the nation, including administrative incompetence, usually determine American presidential elections. This volume confirms the pattern for the November 2024 presidential election. It has revealed that although America faces existential domestic and foreign threats, Kamala Harris and Donald Trump brush core challenges under the rug, striving to beguile rather than educate the electorate. A Harris victory will accelerate the elite privileged, anti-competitive left-wing "straitjacket society" tied to entitlement, affirmative action, egalitarianism, anti-meritocracy, and restorative justice on the home front, and will spur reckless, underfunded sphere of influence wars abroad.

Progressivism began innocuously enough as a series of policies, but has morphed into an over-controlling, anti-competitive, authoritarian revolutionary system drifting toward red Cuban style rationing and anti-plutocratic business restrictions that will not fade quietly into the night. Elite activists will fight rather than switch.

Populism reflects the deep disgruntlement of the productive working class in search of a constructive, institutionally viable vision and road map. Although witheringly attacked by progressives, Project 2025 marks the start of a process for shaping a sustainable competitive populist movement. A Trump victory will provide populism with the foundation required for the restoration of competitive equal opportunity and traditional values. Defeat will propel the Republican Party in hazy new directions.

Both sides bill the November 2024 American presidential election as "existential." They are right.